In spirit…a story of friendship

Amy O'Keeffe

THIS MUST BE THE PLACE (NAIVE MELODY)
Words and Music by DAVID BYRNE CHRIS FRANTZ, JERRY HARRISON and TINA WEYMOUTH
© 1983 WB MUSIC CORP. and INDEX MUSIC, INC.
All rights administered by WB MUSIC CORP.
All Rights Reserved
Used By Permission of ALFRED MUSIC

In Spirit Press

For Grace, my beautiful daughter and cosmic twin

WITH DEEPEST GRATITUDE

After writing a book that took over 20 years to complete, there are so many people to thank. I wouldn't have the opportunity to celebrate the completion of my book, if it weren't for the many angels that made it possible. Thank you from the bottom of my heart to those who read drafts one, two, three and several iterations afterwards, as this story continued to evolve. To those who have been in my life since the beginning of this story, to those who I met along the way, who are just as much a part of it. "Life is not about the clock, but the compass," are great words of wisdom I heard along my journey. I am so grateful to Spirit, God, and this Universe for blessing me with the journey of a lifetime.

Thank you, Char Keane, Jane Zaug (Mom), Miranda Ehmke, Dea Shandera, Michelle Rebek, Jenniffer Weigel, Therese Rowley, Clare Kunkel, Lana Gits, Kathy Worthington, Kate Peterson, Kathleen McAllister, Dessi Keane, Maura Owens Kownacki and for every other editor extraordinaire who blessed me with their time, talent and guidance. In Spirit is because of you.

CONTENTS

PREFACE

One day, when I was twenty-one years old, I was struck with an epiphany. I no longer wanted pain and sadness to consume my soul. In a moment, I realized the anguish I felt within wasn't because of my childhood as I had thought. It wasn't because of the things in life I thought I was missing. It wasn't because of the dreams I hadn't yet reached. That day I heard the voice of my spirit.

It is our spirit that interprets personal revelation, communicates beyond words and feels He or She that is God. Our spirit is the voice of the dreams we have, the intuition we feel, and the desire within us that inspires us to grow. The purpose of life, I realized, is to learn, expand our consciousness, and to experience the extraordinary. As I began to see my life as a journey guided by my spirit, I was transformed. This did not happen in one singular moment, but through a process spanning many moments and many years. I was fortunate to meet someone who shared this journey with me.

Through the gift of an unexpected friendship, painful experiences became joyful lessons, mysteries were contemplated, and miracles happened ...

My first memory of my friend Patty was in the 8th grade on the first day of school. Both of us had recently moved to a small suburb outside of Chicago and transferred into the same Catholic school. I remember Patty being one of the first classmates I noticed. She, like me, was standing awkwardly alone among hundreds of overly excited students, all of whom had known each other for the past eight years of their grammar school life. It took about one minute for me to decide to walk up to Patty and introduce myself. "Are you new here?" I asked her, hoping "yes" would be the answer. I had already determined that she was in the same boat I was, and we were going to get through this terrifying experience together.

I soon found out that Patty and her family just moved back to Chicago after spending the last five years in Dallas, Texas. Even though she attended this school from first through third grade before moving to Dallas, I knew she felt as out of place as I did. Unfortunately, after eagerly comparing our class schedules, we discovered we were assigned to different homerooms. The sound of the first morning bell abruptly ended our conversation, and once again Patty and I were on our own.

Luckily, as the year moved forward, Patty and I settled into our new school and found our own circle of friends. It wasn't until spring of that year that Patty and I were finally given an opportunity to share a class together. We were both required to take a special course in preparation for our Confirmation. Only three of us were there, since most of our classmates were confirmed the year before. Patty and I sat next to each other as we were told what it means to be blessed with the Holy Spirit. According to the

Catholic faith, the sacrament of Confirmation signifies the beginning of your relationship with God.

Our weekly classes began in March. During our third week of class, Sister Anastasia (our teacher and school principal) asked Patty how her father was doing. It was a question that caught my attention. I was unaware that anything was wrong with Patty's dad. I gathered from her conversation with Sister Anastasia that her dad was in the hospital. Patty briefly explained that her dad was feeling much better and he would be home in a few days. Since Patty hadn't shared this news about her dad with me, I felt uncomfortable listening to their conversation. As she and Sister continued to discuss it, I wanted to say something to Patty, but I also didn't want to intrude. Before I could decide what to do, Sister asked us to turn to our books and began discussing our current lesson.

After class, Patty and I walked back to our homerooms, talking about how we would complete the community service hours that were due by the end of the month. As part of our requirements to make Confirmation, we had to complete a certain number of hours of volunteer work. As we continued talking, I went back and forth trying to decide if I should mention anything to Patty about her dad. I didn't want to upset her by bringing up the conversation again. I knew how distraught I would be if I were in Patty's shoes. As Patty and I finally parted ways to go to our respective homerooms, I gave her a friendly wave good-bye and uttered the words under my breath, "I hope your dad feels better soon."

The next day, the entire school assembled into church to participate in an all-school mass. As I walked to church with the rest of my classmates, I remember noticing what a beautiful spring morning it was. It was the end of March and the long Chicago winter had finally let go. The trees were beginning to bud and there wasn't a cloud in the sky. About 15 minutes into mass, Patty's teacher suddenly motioned to her that she needed to leave. I watched as Patty got up and a nun escorted her out of church. Many of our classmates noticed this, and you could hear the whispers as each of us tried to figure out where Patty might be going. Maybe, I wondered, was Patty's dad being released from the hospital and she going home to see him?

After mass, we were sent back to our classrooms. Those of us who knew Patty continued to discuss why she left so abruptly. Since no one else knew that Patty's dad was in the hospital, some suggested that she probably had to leave early for an appointment, or perhaps she just wasn't feeling well. I, too, eventually believed that this must have been the case. But by the look on our teacher's face when she shut the door of our homeroom, I knew it had to be something else. Our teacher informed us that, while in the hospital, Patty's dad had suffered a massive heart attack and died that morning.

Throughout grammar school and high school, the personal and painful experience of Patty's father's death was a subject she kept mostly to herself. As the years passed by, our conversations mostly centered on who we hoped to go to homecoming with and why they hadn't asked us yet. The summer of our junior year in high school, I remember spending countless days with Patty just hanging out together in the basement of the home I grew up in, or long afternoons at the neighborhood pool. We would take turns discussing the dramas of our summer crushes as we played the song, "Turn A Different Corner" by George Michael over and over again. Mostly though, Patty and I spent much of our time laughing. I grew to know her as one of the funniest and most outrageous people I had ever met. I related to her sense of adventure and enjoyed nothing more than joining her in something that we weren't supposed to be doing! Like the time Patty, our friend Michelle, and I drove across two states from Illinois to Ohio and back in less than 24 hours to get fake IDs—which, of course, were taken away from us the very first time we tried to use them. Nevertheless, the adventure was worth the ride.

It wasn't until the end of college that a turning point occurred. Patty and Michelle were attending Marquette University in Wisconsin and I had come for a weekend visit. Michelle had an event to attend that weekend, so Patty invited me over to her sorority house to visit with her. It was a late Saturday afternoon and we spent the time just hanging out and catching up while Patty cleaned her bedroom. It was also the first time in a while that we had the chance to really talk. Eventually, we found ourselves talking about the day Patty's father died. It was the first time we discussed how deeply that experience had affected Patty. Before we knew it, three hours had passed. Patty talked about how she felt from the moment she heard the news that her dad had died, to how hard it was to live the last eight years without him. I suddenly understood a part of Patty that I didn't know before.

That day I, too, shared some of my own painful family experiences that I had never talked about with friends. Because of the pain that Patty had endured, it felt right to share my experiences with her. It was hard to explain to outsiders what my home life was like. I was the oldest of five children and despite our tumultuous home life, my four siblings, mother and I had managed to portray our family experience as loving, fun and normal as any family of seven with two dogs and two cats can.

During my teenage years, our family lived in an affluent neighborhood, had a beautiful home, and everything—materially—we could have wanted. It hadn't always been that way. For the first eleven years of my life, it was a constant struggle for us financially. Not only financially, but my father, for lack of a better description, was a total raging maniac. My mother was a cross between a saint and a reincarnation of Lucille Ball. Everyone who knew her loved her. Our household was either amid a violent seize of insanity or a hilarious scene straight out of the movie, *Freaky Friday*.

Unfortunately, even after my dad changed careers, and regardless of the many opportunities my family and I were now afforded, my siblings and mother and I lived in day to day fear. My dad's constant outbursts of irrational anger had nothing to do with a lack of love for us, as he told each one of us "I love you" every day of our lives. And I believe that he did. However, as much pride as my dad took in being a father, the demons from his own childhood had become part of our family dynamic. His demons caused me to feel both loved and hated by him, and I never knew which side of him was going to show up at the dinner table.

Back in Patty's sorority's house that afternoon, we both found ourselves saying to each other, "I never knew that about you." Before putting it into words, neither Patty nor I realized what we'd been through. As I left Patty's sorority house that night, I felt as though I had just finished an intense therapy session. It was so unexpected, and, at the same time, our conversation felt like an answer to a prayer.

Following college graduation, Patty planned to continue living in Milwaukee. Michelle and her college roommates, Dara and Cathy, would be living there as well. Cathy and Patty had rented an apartment together in the same area where Dara and

Michelle had rented a place. I was still in school, living in Chicago with another grade-school friend named Allison. By the end of college—and several road trips from Chicago to Milwaukee later—Allison, Cathy, Dara, Michelle, Patty and I had formed a special bond. We had no better fun than when we were together.

With Allison and I living in Chicago and the rest of the girls living in Milwaukee, all of us anticipated a summer of many visits. However, at the beginning of that summer, a small twist of fate abruptly changed our plans. While transporting the glass top of a table, Patty dropped it and broke her foot. Patty and I later joked that it was her broken foot that gave us the opportunity to become the best of friends.

Since Patty couldn't get around easily on her own, she moved back home for the summer to the suburbs where both of our families lived. Soon after Patty returned home, we went to lunch together and began discussing our plans for the summer. Our options weren't looking very promising. It was then that Patty and I came up with the idea that we would try to spend as much time as we could at my family's vacation house near Lake Geneva, Wisconsin.

Whenever we could, the girls and I would go there. Whether it was summer, winter, spring or fall, we spent time in Lake Geneva, hanging out and laughing constantly. Our days there would always consist of making an amazing dinner paired with several bottles of cheap white zinfandel. A cup of Irish Cream-flavored coffee always followed, no matter what the hour, and then we'd make our way to Chuck's, the local lakeside bar.

During our college years, the girls and I felt as close as friends who had been together for a lifetime. I had spent many years of my childhood going to Lake Geneva with my family. My parents eventually bought a home there during my senior year of high school. Instantly, I regarded it as my own. There was no other place in the world that I felt more at home. Since my family didn't go there often, it was place that had become a sanctuary for the girls and me.

As Patty and I continued to discuss our plans, I told her I would help her "hobble around" on her broken foot. We were both excited, but still somewhat unsure about what to expect. In truth, we had never spent much time together without the other girls. But the more we talked about it, the more we looked forward to our plans. Patty reminded me of the graduation card I had recently given to her, where I wrote, "I hope that we become a special part of each other's lives." I had been inspired by the conversation she and I shared at her sorority house just a few months before. "Something told me that we would be," I said to her. "Now here we are," she replied. We believed we were brought together for a reason.

That reason became apparent the very first time we drove to Lake Geneva that summer. During the first hour of our drive, Patty and I poured our souls out to each other. It was part II of our conversation at her sorority house. We soon felt a sense of familiarity with each other that neither of us had known before. We spoke the same language. There was a powerful bond we soon felt between us that not only came from many of the experiences we related to, but also in the way we understood each other.

We continued our drive and conversation, finally turning off the highway and onto the beautiful Wisconsin country roads. From this vantage point, there was a cluster of black clouds looming in the western sky and before we knew it, we were driving through a blinding thunderstorm. At any other time, I would have been gripped in fear by the scene around me, but Patty and I saw it as something else. We were convinced that the incredible force of nature around us was simply a reflection of the amazing conversation that was taking place between us.

We made our way back and forth several times to Lake Geneva that summer. Each time we learned something more about each other—including our discovered talent for playing pool, which became one of our favorite evening pastimes at Chuck's. I was also learning things about myself. I felt a sense of inner guidance I had never known before. Something told me that there was so much more to know about life than what I was experiencing: that it was time to look forward and stop looking back. And if I had the courage to walk the journey, I would find myself where I wanted to be. The same voice told me it would guide me every step of the way. Both Patty and I recognized that inner voice as the voice of our spirits. We believed that together we had embarked on a kind of spiritual journey. What we didn't know then was that we were about to discover what that really meant.

Patty and I decided to rent an apartment together in Chicago, just down the street from Wrigley Field on Waveland Avenue. We were both 23. We took our first "real jobs" and were ecstatic to be living in the heart of the city. Later, when Patty and I would recall that time, we referred to it as our "Waveland Experience." It was a life-changing time for both of us.

Even though Patty and I were different in many ways, we were the same when it came to our enthusiastic and positive demeanor. We seemed to mirror each other's sense of expressiveness and supportiveness. Patty attached the word "fabulous" to just about everything I said or did. Her encouragement touched a place within me that I never knew I needed. In the most powerful way, it felt more like healing.

Soon we developed a tradition of congregating at our kitchen table. It was here we discussed everything from the mundane activities of our work days to our hopes for our lives. Our kitchen table had become our sacred place where we held meetings of the minds, acted as therapists for each other, and laughed out loud late into the night before realizing that we were never going to wake up for work on time. Patty and I had suddenly become experts in the art of listening as we allowed each other to work through each of our own our life lessons.

At the end of any one of our talks, we were there for each other to say, "I commend your courage, thank you for listening, and you are fantastic!" And before I could criticize myself for any awkward turns taken or regrettable choices made, Patty would stop me in my tracks by telling me, "I am amazed by your strength." For the first time in my life, I felt strong because of my experiences. Patty once wrote to me, "You always inspire me to find the experience in life!" It is something we did for each other.

We learned to see life as a spiritual experience because we knew we were evolving. That year our mission in life was to face our fears and experience the exhilaration that comes when you do. I didn't want to be afraid anymore. I was determined to live a different life than the one I had been living. For the first time in my life, I felt a true sense of courage.

That year, I became aware of myself as a spiritual being. I saw the universe as a friendly and powerful place. Both Patty and I related to everything in terms of energy. Whatever we give we get more of, what we appreciate multiplies, and whatever we choose to know in life becomes our reality, were spiritual principles that Patty and I began to recognize. We came to believe that the spiritual lessons we were seeking to understand in life were seeking us.

The year before Patty and I moved into our apartment on Waveland, I was reading the book *The Return to Love* by Marianne Williamson, which my mom insisted I read. In the book, Williamson reflects on a work called *A Course in Miracles*, which was originally written by two agnostic professors at Columbia University who give full authorship to the Holy Spirit. The theme of the book that hit home for me was the idea that when in doubt, despair, anger or fear, you pray to the Holy Spirit for a miracle to heal your thoughts. The miracle is the sudden ability to change your perception regarding a circumstance or feeling that once caused you pain. In other words, you see things differently—and the result is a shift in your thoughts, which transforms all things.

Although I was skeptical that a book could offer me any meaningful guidance, I agreed to read it. As much as I aspired to live an enlightened life, I was struggling to leave the past behind. The painful and traumatic memories from my childhood at times were all consuming. In many ways, I felt broken. Growing up, I always knew my home life was insane. It was a way of life. Living on my own, I realized I didn't have to live one more day of it.

By the end of the first chapter, I couldn't put the book down. I spent the entire year reading and re-reading it. According to the book, by praying to the Holy Spirt for a miracle, your entire life will change. As challenging as it was for me to believe this, my heart was telling me it was true. This book was not about the Holy Spirit, God or any miracles I was taught while growing up. As the book suggested, I began praying to the Holy Spirit for miracles. Whenever I felt any sense of anxiety, fear or uncertainty, I would pray for a shift in my perception—or a miracle, as the book called it.

Things did begin to change. I changed. For the first time in my life, I realized it was my choice to heal—or not. The way we perceive our experiences is a choice. As much as I believed I was entitled to live in a constant state of sadness, based on certain experiences I'd been through, I knew I had to let go of them if I wanted to be happy. I was learning things on a spiritual level I had never experienced before. As I saw it, everything from my painful past, to the fears I now wanted to face, offered an opportunity to learn more.

It was also the first time I had thought about the Holy Spirit since my eighth-grade Confirmation. Thirteen years ago, as I sat next to Patty, I was told about, "the promise of the Holy Spirit." But only now did I begin to understand its meaning. I couldn't help but think that Patty and I were brought together back then and now to help each other heal. Life had come full circle. For someone who had, for the most part, left religion behind, I was suddenly in awe of the power of God.

Patty and I, in the meantime, were also having the most fun of our lives. I recall countless times that made us laugh, and the memories come to life again as I remember them now. When I close my eyes, I hear our voices, always with a tone of excitement saying, "What's next?" Both Patty and I felt a sense of confidence and fearlessness that we both longed to know.

My memories while living on Waveland Avenue consist of the endless conversations Patty and I had at our kitchen table: the weekday mornings when I would be in a mad dash scurrying around our apartment getting ready for work, only to see Patty running out the door with a pair of nylons in her hands, late for the train; bawling our eyes out during any sad movie until we burst into laughter; our Thursday night ritual of watching "Seinfeld" before we went out for "dollar beer night" at the Cubby Bear; having all the girls spend the night at our apartment during the summer, sleeping in every square inch of space; sweating in what we referred to as our "hot box inferno;" Patty and I laughing at each other for the concoctions we dressed ourselves in to survive Chicago's winters; singing along with the radio at the top of our lungs in Patty's car; making it our mission to be in the front row of any concert we attended; hearing Patty's laughter from 20 feet away, and without even knowing what was funny, laughing myself; sharing our stories of the day before we went to sleep; making Patty laugh just as she was taking a drink of something; running along the lakefront together after work and celebrating our annual Christmas get-together where the girls and I would exchange grab bag gifts, enjoying a tradition we held so dear dedicated to our friendship.

Most of all, I remember a promise that Patty and I made to each other. While shopping at one of the boutiques in our neighborhood, I bought the most beautiful red rose and bright yellow sunflower that were hair accessories. (This was before the big sunflower trend, so I especially thought the sunflower was unique.) I always kept the sunflower and the rose next to each other as a decoration on my dresser. Whenever I chose to wear one of the flowers in my hair, I would choose the rose. One day, Patty asked me if she could borrow the sunflower, which she planned to pin to one of her many blazers. She pinned it on the lapel of her jacket, so it would be sure to stand out. Whenever Patty wore the sunflower, her co-workers would tell her how much they loved it. They told her it was so perfect for her.

"Everyone says it makes them smile," Patty told me.

"You can borrow it anytime you want," I responded. "On second thought, you should have it. If it makes the people who see you wear it smile, then that's what it's meant to do."

"Are you sure?" Patty asked, touched by the offer.

"Absolutely!" I replied.

As I gave Patty the sunflower, a thought came to me. "I know, you be the sunflower and I'll be the rose," I said as I handed it to her.

Patty agreed that it was the perfect symbol for each of us. "That's how we'll always remember each other," she said.

"Whenever one of us sees a sunflower or a rose, we'll know it's a sign of the other," I replied.

We both agreed that it was something we would always remember.

Those days living on Waveland Avenue felt like a quest for light. Light that brings perspective and clarity—and energetically draws you to the experiences, people and places deep within your soul you are meant to connect with. Patty and I realized we were brought together to help each other learn. One night, after one of our special talks at the kitchen table, Patty and I summed it up by writing on a piece of paper, "Some things have been discovered, some things have been healed, some things forgotten, and some things revealed." We knew we were meant to learn more.

One gorgeously sunny, warm Sunday morning in August, I woke up early and knew I had to wake Patty up immediately. The air and sky were so awesome that I felt like we shouldn't waste another minute inside. After easily convincing Patty, we walked out of our apartment half-dressed, with undone hair and a dab of lipstick. Next, we hopped in her car and headed to the lakefront. We arrived at a place along the shoreline we referred to as "the rocks," where huge boulders are perpetually hit by the crashing waves from Lake Michigan.

I remember that morning so well—the light of the sun sparkled like a million diamonds dancing across the water. As Patty and I stood looking out over the water, I felt completely at peace. I could feel Patty's energy united with mine. That morning, as we both looked across the horizon from the edge of those rocks, we sat in silence taking in the view. I grabbed my camera and took a picture to remember the moment. Something told me that this was the final scene for this part of our journey. Intuitively, it was something we both knew. We were ready to move on. We were ready to ride the wave of light—not just look at it from the shore. Later that day, while we were walking down our block, we ran into a guy we knew who randomly asked us if we would sublet our apartment to him. Without hesitation, we turned to each other and said, "Let's do it!"

Luckily, Patty and I had a friend who was living in a two-flat that had a vacant first floor, so we had a place to move to. It was further up north along the lake. It had three bedrooms, two bathrooms, a sunroom, dishwasher, hardwood floors, stained glass windows, sunlight everywhere, free gated parking and the cheapest rent in town. Patty and I were sure we had found heaven. We were elated with our "new palace" and the possibilities that lay ahead. Life had presented us with a different space in which to grow—and we were thrilled for the opportunity. We decided to think big and be open to a different plan, a "higher" plan.

Much like our morning at the rocks, we were ready to "ride the wave."

*   *   *

It was the fall of 1994, although the season was more like a long stretch of Indian summer. The thought of winter felt years away. One warm September night, as I was sitting outside of our new apartment enjoying the soft breeze of the evening air, I remember feeling acutely aware of the present moment. I didn't want to let go of it. Even though we had settled into our new home, I could sense something in the Universe was still changing for Patty and me. The idea of this felt intriguing and something I looked forward to. Even so, that night I realized not to take this time for granted.

As Patty and I had done for the past year since becoming roommates, we created new rituals while living in our new apartment. One of our favorites was sitting on our sun porch on the weekend fall mornings with a hot cup of coffee as the bright morning light poured through the stained-glass windows. Since our previous apartment had little to no sunlight, we were thrilled. It was as if we were on vacation in a place we'd never been before. It never took long before we'd decide we wanted to get out and do something. We'd get dressed, grab a paper and pen, our favorite music and head to the car. Our only plan, which we did almost every Sunday that fall, would be to drive north along the lakefront on Sheridan Road where life always demonstrated its magic.

We'd figure out where our destination would be when we got there. Sometimes we'd find ourselves in a town we'd never been to—or at the Chicago Botanic Gardens or Plaza Del Lago, where we would browse through the shops and stop for a mocha at an Italian café. The best part of the trip was getting there. Patty and I were unencumbered by the need to create any kind of plan. Our only intention was to allow our minds to wander and enjoy the beautiful day. There was no better view than the winding road that bordered Lake Michigan, which looked as enormous and blue as any ocean. The relaxed pace of a Sunday, the brilliant sunshine, vibrant colored leaves and soft September air made it the perfect drive. There was nothing more that Patty and I loved to do than drive with the windows down, with the sun shining down our faces and our favorite music blasting from our car. Along the way, without fail, we would turn to each other at the same moment and utter, "amazing." As if by coincidence, a song would play on the radio that described everything we felt at that moment. I remember the song called, "Dreams," by the Cranberries that always seemed to play. We knew then the Universe was in tune with us.

The Universe continued to guide us later that Fall during the last time we went to Lake Geneva. It was the first time we had been there since my parents had sold our home there the month before. It was the first of many changes that were happening, whether I was ready for them or not. Having to sell this house that I loved so much was not sitting well with me.

The chill of November was settling in, so the girls and I decided to meet each other for the weekend in Lake Geneva. We decided to stay at one of the local motels on the outskirts of town. It wouldn't be the same without our "retreat house," but I was still looking forward to being in Lake Geneva with my friends.

As always, we had a great time together that weekend. It felt so good just to be together. We took a drive around the lake, and for nostalgia's sake, we decided to drive into the subdivision of my former house. We parked in front of it with loud music and chatter emanating from the car. I would have given anything just to be able to walk through the front door. It felt surreal to think that I no longer could. I thought about how much I missed my house until I realized something else: it wasn't the house that created those moments, it was us.

The next morning, we decided to stop for breakfast in town before making our way home. Patty and I were lagging, so the other girls went ahead to get a table at the restaurant. After getting my things together, I stepped out of our motel room to check out the weather. It was a chilly, cloudy morning. I told Patty that I would wait for her in the car. As I sat in the driver's seat, I noticed that the door to the room next to ours was open. I saw a middle-aged, nicely dressed woman who appeared to be packing her things. I watched her walk to her minivan, which was parked next to our car and begin loading it with her bags. After taking several trips back and forth from her room to her car, I watched as she tried dragging out one of the biggest suitcases I had ever seen. Eventually she noticed me, and we both smiled and gave each other a little wave.

Besides Patty and I, this woman appeared to be the only person staying at the motel. I couldn't help but wonder what she was doing there. For a moment I thought that she might be visiting someone. But then why would she be staying at this motel? Since it was a Sunday, I didn't get the feeling that she was on a business trip. It also seemed odd to me that she would be vacationing alone in the middle of November.

I was anxious for a cup of coffee, so I was relieved when I saw Patty close the door to our room and make her way to our car. I figured we would talk about the curious woman on the way to the restaurant.

The woman shut the trunk of her car just as Patty was shutting the door to our room. As they passed each other in the parking lot, they said hello to each other. The next thing I knew, their hello turned into a 30-minute conversation. At first I thought it was interesting that Patty might know what this woman was doing and where she was going. After another 10 minutes passed, I became annoyed. I couldn't figure out what the hell they could be talking about. "I hope they're not just having a nice chat while I'm sitting here," I thought to myself. Then another 15 minutes went by. I had to use some self-control not to roll down the window and yell, "Come on!" I wondered if the girls would even still be at the restaurant. Was Patty enjoying this conversation? Maybe this woman was crazy, and Patty couldn't find a way to break away. From the look I saw on Patty's face, I could see that this wasn't the case. There had to be a very good reason why Patty would be standing in the freezing cold, talking to a perfect stranger while the rest of us were waiting for her. I told myself to be patient for the third time since I'd been sitting there.

At last, Patty and the woman gave each other a long hug goodbye and flashed me an apologetic smile. I smiled back, of course, gesturing to them that it was okay. At this point, the only thing I was thinking about was getting a cup of coffee.

"You're not going to believe this," Patty said to me as she got in the car. I was already driving out of the parking lot like a mad woman.

"I hope I won't," I said sarcastically.

Patty reminded me of something that we saw on television on Halloween night just a few weeks before. There had been a horrible rainstorm with massive wind gusts. It was so windy that I could barely open the back gate of our apartment. It was a night that for some reason, I continued to think back on, even before Patty reminded me about it.

That night, as Patty and I sat sprawled out in our living room watching television, a news brief aired in between the movie we were watching. A small commercial plane carrying Chicago passengers had crashed in the middle of a field in Indiana. Every person on the plane had been killed. We kept checking different television stations to learn more about this tragic story. The rain was blowing hard on the reporters who were trying to piece together the facts of the plane crash. They didn't give the names of the victims because their family members hadn't been notified. As it turned out, this woman's husband had been one of the passengers killed in the plane crash.

She initially told Patty that she was lost. She didn't know where she was going. Even though she had grown children and a family to support her through her tragedy, she just needed to go somewhere alone. I instinctively felt that she found Patty because Patty was a gifted listener.

It's one of those random events that isn't random at all. Something very important happened to this woman and Patty after their exchange. The woman's son called Patty six months later when he found the business card she had given to his mother. He wanted to thank Patty for talking to his mom, and to let her know that his mother still talked about their conversation and how much it meant to her. As her son explained, it helped bring his mom home in more ways than one.

Their exchange helped Patty come to terms with the loss of her father 10 years earlier. Patty hadn't been able to step inside a church, hospital or any other public place without feeling the pain of that memory. Supporting someone else in her grief, allowed Patty to realize where she was with her own. Their conversation helped Patty to finally begin to make peace with her pain.

A month later, Patty found herself, once again, faced with a similar circumstance. She worked in the benefits department at a national bank and received a phone call from a woman named Lynn who was concerned about her benefits. It was a conversation that struck Patty immediately as she listened in awe to this woman's situation. Lynn was in her late thirties and dying of cancer. She had a son and a daughter, ages 13 and 14—the same ages Patty and her brother John were when their father died.

Patty called me at work later that day and asked me to meet her for dinner. She said she wanted to share the story from beginning to end about her conversation with a woman named Lynn, with whom she had never spoken.

Initially, Patty was trying to help Lynn with the questions she had about her benefits. Because of the sensitivity of Lynn's situation, Patty kept her on the phone as she searched for as much information as she could. As they spoke, Patty and Lynn connected on a more personal level. It was a conversation that went on for hours.

Patty said she and Lynn talked, laughed and cried together. They shared who they were as people. They talked about life. They became friends. They talked about what it feels like to know that you are dying and what it feels like to lose those you love. Lynn wanted to know from Patty's perspective what she could do to help her children deal with her imminent death. Patty shared her point of view as a child who had lost a parent and all the things that would be most important to Lynn's children as they learned to cope without her. It was everything that Patty had needed to hear herself when her dad died.

Lynn told Patty that talking with her that day had made it one of the best days of her life. Patty was equally touched by their conversation and was in awe of their profound connection. It was an experience that changed them both deeply.

When Patty and I met for dinner later that night, we discussed how it might have been possible that Lynn could have reached any number of employees who worked in Patty's department. We both agreed that receiving Lynn's call was no coincidence. Nothing ever is.

"Shotgun Down the Avalanche." These words remind me of New Year's Eve, 1994. A new year was about to make its entrance—and impact—on my life. "Shotgun Down the Avalanche" is the name of a song by Shawn Colvin that Patty and I had been listening to for the past two years straight. As a matter of fact, we listened to it that day singing our hearts out loudly along with it just as we always did. To me, the song described what it means when the forces of life take you through an experience that is out of your control. Patty and I took the lyrics of the song literally, as we believed we were riding down the "avalanches" in our own lives side by side.

I thought about that song again as I stared up at the stars in Crested Butte, Colorado. I had traveled there with Patty and Allison from Copper Mountain, Colorado, a ski resort town where Patty, Allison and I were staying with friends of Patty's family for their annual holiday ski trip. Crested Butte was a quaint, artsy town surrounded by the most heavenly beauty on earth.

We risked our lives getting there through several treacherous mountain roads. The situation was most apparent as we drove over one mountain pass, thousands of feet high during a snowstorm. (I happened to be the one driving our mid-sized Saturn rental car, which we mistakenly thought was a good choice for driving in the Colorado Rockies!) We spent over an hour driving up and then down a narrow, icy road through heavily falling snow, going 15 miles per hour. My hands were clenched to the steering wheel the entire time. For the most part, Allison, Patty and I remained calm. However, there wasn't a moment during our drive when we weren't holding our breath. Once we began to make our final decent down the mountain pass, I wasn't sure how this ride was going to end. I kept my foot resting lightly on the brakes as we tried coasting our way down. Based on the steep decline, there were times when I needed to put more pressure on the brakes to keep us from picking up speed. Every time I had to do this, I could feel myself shaking, and the three of us would curse under our breath. My strategy for keeping things under control, both inside the car and out, was working until the brakes of the car suddenly locked. After several failed attempts to gain control on the ice, the engine died. But our car continued moving! It began to pick up speed as we descended the mountain pass. I had no idea what we should do next. The three of us were now cursing out loud.

If I turned the wheel to the right, we would hit the rock in the side of the mountain. If I turned left, we would be in danger of driving off the cliff. There were no guardrails to prevent us from crashing to the bottom of the mountain pass some thousands of feet below. If we were lucky, a 200-year-old evergreen might cushion our plunge. We were all speechless. Our hearts were thumping out of our chests. I had no idea what to do.

"Let go," a voice said to me.

"Let go! Let go of what!" I wanted to know.

The voice in my head continued. "You don't have a choice and you're not going to get out of this otherwise."

"OK," I whispered to myself. This was probably not the time to relax, but that's the message I heard as clear as day.

As the car moved faster, heading downward without the use of brakes, I took a breath and, in fact, did nothing.

"Shift the car into neutral," I heard a split second later.

"Now turn the ignition over." Thank the Lord, the car started!

"Now brake, softly." Hallelujah! We were saved.

I was amazed that I had the ability to surrender my fear. I pictured us spinning out of control down that Godforsaken mountain pass, which should have been closed hours before! What would have happened if I hadn't "let go?"

Back to New Year's Eve -- I was feeling nostalgic and sentimental about the past year as I stood alone looking up at the Colorado sky, minutes before midnight. I asked the Universe and the God who saved my life earlier that day what, if anything, the stars held for me. Although I couldn't put my finger on it, I felt a sense of unease in my gut. I tried to shake off this feeling and instead focus my thoughts on the experiences of the past year. Life had changed for the better on so many levels. I hoped that it was only the beginning of more good things to come in the new year. I said a prayer for the year's blessings and walked into the camper where Patty, Allison and Patty's friend, Bob, who we had to come to visit, were ringing in the New Year.

"Happy New Year!" We all cheered and hugged. Earlier in the evening, we had all been feeling lethargic. Even though we thought it would be fun to ring in the New Year with the locals at one of Crested Butte's quaint local bars, none of them seemed to be calling to us. I was just as glad because I loved and would always remember, my moment of bonding with the Universe at midnight. However, once we rang in the new year just the four of us, we were all ready and excited to hit the town.

Just before we left, Patty handed me a folded piece of paper and said, "Look, this was the Christmas card Bob sent out this year."

I was taken aback as I stood looking at Bob's card. The picture on the cover was a character figure looking up at the Colorado night sky in front of the mountains staring at one bright star with the lyrics from the song "This Must Be The Place," by the group, The Talking Heads written on the bottom of the card.

Patty and I played this song as we traveled on the way to this mountaintop. I recorded it on a tape that I had made especially for our trip to Colorado. It was one of those songs that resonated with me so deeply, but I couldn't say why.

There were many experiences that I couldn't quite explain during our time in Colorado. The beauty was mystifying. Patty and I both were so inspired by it. At one point during our drive back from Crested Butte to Copper Mountain, Patty impulsively pulled over to the side of the road. I didn't need to ask her what she was doing because I already knew. Patty wanted to stop and just look. After parking the car, she, Allison and I just sat there silently, staring into the horizon at the brightest sun I'd ever seen. Something within me felt as big as the scene I was looking at. We drove away realizing that there was so much more to see.

It was our trip to Colorado that inspired Patty to move there. She had traveled to the mountains several times during family ski trips, but only this time did she experience her life and those mountains in a different way. She shared with me what she wrote in her journal after returning from Crested Butte on January 1, 1995--- the moment her decision to move became clear.

"Driving through the mountains, I was blessed. I felt, I explored, and I wondered-

in awe of the world around me. I read about another place. Now I am here. I spend 10 hours a day focusing on one subject. I do it well, too well. I now can see that there should never be one subject.

"I let the scenes roll through my head ... unorganized thoughts. I find no need to put them in their proper order. I want them to roll on. This place allows my focus to be within. I can see that today. And I am happy.

Thank you…"

I was so impressed with Patty's courage to follow through with something she knew was right for her. Even though it wasn't an easy decision, Patty was prepared to move to Colorado—no matter what. The most difficult part for her was telling certain family members and friends that she was moving to a place where she knew no one, had no place to live, and no job lined up. It was hard enough convincing herself she was doing the right thing, let alone anyone else. Patty was also concerned about leaving her position at the bank. She didn't want to disappoint anyone who counted on her. Neither her family nor her friends would be happy to see her go, but we all knew how important it was to support her decision.

Patty and I had spent the last two years of our lives learning to trust our inner voices, knowing there was a reason behind every choice we were inspired to make. We soon realized those years were preparing us for something bigger. The only thing left to do now was to "take the chance" as we used to say and do it. I felt like I had a rock in the pit of my stomach the day that Patty left, but there was nothing more I wanted to do than support her. We counted on that from each other.

I tried to find the perfect words of inspiration to give to Patty as she set forth on her new journey. I included in a card a quote I'd recently read that struck me:

"If you bring forth what is within you, what you bring forth will save you. If you do not bring forth what is within you, what you do not bring forth will destroy you," as attributed to Jesus Christ in the Gospel of Thomas.

That winter seemed to last an eternity. I, too, left my secure corporate job to "take a chance" and give up what no longer felt right for me. Quitting my job and creating a new life in the dead of winter in Chicago wasn't quite as inspiring as I had hoped. As I found out, it's a struggle to maintain your sense of self-worth and enthusiasm when you're unemployed and you haven't a clue what your next move should be. However, I was determined not to be, as my friends and I like to say, "thrown over the edge." It became my mountain to climb that winter—in addition to going through the separation anxiety of missing my best friend.

I knew I had to look within myself to find the positive support that I was used to receiving from Patty. Like Patty, I wanted to pursue the unknown and explore a more creative way to make a living. In time, I believed the answer would appear and the opportunities I desired would fall into my lap. However, that belief was often overshadowed by self-doubt. I soon began to feel like a total loser—and totally screwed.

Deep down, I believed I was going through what I was meant to go through. In the end, I knew that Patty and I would analyze and deconstruct every situation, and together we would find the sacred truth behind my learning experience. These were our favorite types of conversations to have—ones I couldn't wait to share again with her, face to face. So, after hearing that Patty planned to come home for a week, the first week of

May, I was ecstatic. I was not only thrilled for her visit, but I was also beginning to feel like myself again after a long, difficult winter. I couldn't wait to share our stories and, together, experience the beginning of spring.

When Patty and I first discussed her visit home, she thought about flying in. However, it didn't take long before we both quickly realized that we would need her car to take part in all our favorite rituals—the first of which would be in our apartment at our dining room table. The very first thing we did after Patty walked through the door of our apartment—after the two of us spent the first 15 minutes jumping up and down with excitement—was plant ourselves at our dining room table in preparation for the purposeful conversations that we knew lay ahead.

After quickly catching up on small talk, Patty wanted to share with me her experience of those first days she traveled to Colorado, as she had written about it in her journal. Previously, we had been keeping "a log" as we referred to it, in a little notebook that Patty dated "September 24, 1994 ... the day we started our log." Our purpose was to record our own reflections and insights, in preparation for the book that we hoped one day to write together. Inspired by that notion, I had given Patty a journal for her 24th birthday. She asked me to read the entry she wrote as she began her journey to Colorado.

"January 25th - Last day of work was Jan 19th. Supposed to leave the 23rd. Left the 24th. Will leave Gram's tomorrow - Not quite sure where I'm heading. Somehow I'll get there. Maybe Denver or Boulder. I'm just not sure.

I feel like crying. What have I done - can't lose courage. Now I'm on my own. John is stopping here. It will feel good I think. I need to call on some people. I need to depend on them. It is O.K. Somehow I'll make it through today.

-Boulder has Tom, Sandy, and Chris

-Denver has Randy

Call 2 jobs

January 26th - I'm not sure what time it is. It's dark -- all I know is I can't sleep anymore. Time to go. This will be my last night in the lap of luxury -- better shower.

Thank you, Grandma, for the quilt - I will cherish it forever. What a good sign, the softening effect of a grandma's quilt... warmth .... Thank you.

4:44 a.m. on Highway 10 ... Windshield wipers going -- no rain -- Leader of the Band playing; feel like crying; maybe I will check the maps one more time -- even though I've traveled these roads a thousand times.

8:19 a.m. Rest Area -- clean enough

I feel better. I followed a crescent moon that miraculously turned into a bright ball of fire staring at me through the rear-view mirror – Thank you!

A rainbow mirage glows around me on the horizon.

Hey, cows! What's going on!

12:10 p.m. Welcome to Colorado

Perfectly content ... listening to Embraced by the Light -- enraptured

I am having a beautiful experience -- I will never forget. The sun is so hot on the left side of my face and arm.

Rest Area #3

I met a beautiful old lady with a babushka -- nothing to say about her, just beautiful. She gave me peace and wished upon me a safe journey. Thank you.

Amy -- you and I had the parents we have and the common experiences, so that one day we would join together in force & positive energy to teach & learn from others

and each other. Now we are still doing that -- only allowing each other to reach further

-- eventually coming together again. We are the base -- soul mates! You are my

special angel. My life was incomplete until I met you. You opened so many doors &

windows letting the fresh air fill my soul.

You are a guardian over that soul you helped to inspire. I don't recognize some

of the years, thoughts, lack thereof the days before I knew and grew with you. Thank you

- Thank you - Thank you...

OH MY GOD -- I was so "embraced" by the light that I ran out of gas -- literally

rolling into the Texaco.

Thank God! EMPTY! Oh My! OOPS, never under estimate the power of fumes!

Where am I?"

After reading Patty's first-hand account of driving to Colorado, I told her how

impressed I was with her courage. "I would have turned back after receiving Grandma's

quilt!" I said to her. She laughed. I also told her that the sentiments she had written in

her journal blew me away. "I am so touched," I told her, wishing I could have put into

better words how much her thoughts meant to me.

"I mean what I wrote," Patty replied.

That night we continued our conversation by catching up on certain stories and

any "learning processes," as we called them, that we both had experienced since Patty left

for Colorado. I was excited to hear that Patty was so moved by the book *Embraced by*

the Light by Betty Eadie. I had read that book the year before and shared what I read with

Patty. She had always enjoyed hearing about any books I was reading, and we would discuss them as if she read them herself.

During Patty's drive to Colorado, she had come across a store that rented books on tape. When she found a copy of *Embraced by the Light,* she told me that she knew it was meant to be. We both agreed that it was the perfect book to accompany her on this trip.

The ideas in the book changed my perspective on many levels. The story was told and inspired by a woman who had been clinically dead for many hours and had experienced the afterlife. I was moved to learn from the author's testimony that in the moments after she died, her spirit immediately went to her loved ones and to those with whom she was close during her life. Through this woman's story, I also learned that our purpose in life is to experience spiritual lessons. As the author stated, before we come to this earth, each of us agrees to everything that we will experience in our lives. We choose our paths to learn spiritual lessons not only for ourselves, but for the spiritual lessons we will teach others.

Patty and I had never discussed what we believed happens when we die. Our Catholic upbringing had taught us that we go to heaven and our souls are no longer connected to the mortal world. I had never questioned this until I read *Embraced by the Light*. Nor had I ever been exposed to the idea that we have anything to do with the lessons we choose to learn when we come to this earth. Patty and I discussed these ideas in depth that night. We were both in awe as we grasped certain concepts we had never considered about life.

On that note, we knew it was time to indulge in one of our other favorite things to do: going out on a Thursday night. We made a point to visit some of our favorite places, as we cruised the city in Patty's car blaring our favorite music, feeling as good as we always did in each other's company. As we began our journey, I put one of my new tapes in the cassette player. I made the tape especially for our new "spring experience" and I couldn't wait for Patty to hear it. Even though we shared different tastes in music, I always knew what she would love. Patty asked me if she could play a song for me instead. It was a song called, "I'll Stand by You," by The Pretenders. Patty said that the song reminded her of our friendship every time she heard it. After we listened to it, Patty turned to me and said, in a voice set apart from her usual lighthearted way, that she would always stand by me no matter what.

"Thank you, I feel the same," I replied with a little lump in my throat. There was something about our exchange that made me feel sad.

"I'll add the song to my tape, so I'll always have it to remember," I told her.

During Patty's visit home that week in May we did everything as if it were the last time. Even the weather cooperated. The transition from the end of winter to the beginning of spring seemed to appear all at once. The sky was blue, the air was warm, and from the scent of lilacs, every lilac tree in the city was in bloom. That week, Patty and I talked endlessly, drove for the sake of driving, saw the perfect movie, ran into old friends and, in between, made each other laugh constantly. We also had the chance to see one of our favorite singers, Mary Black, who was from Ireland. Neither of us had ever seen her perform.

When Patty and I went to buy our tickets to see Mary (on the day of the concert) we found out that the show had just sold out. Although we were disappointed, we were still determined to get tickets. We stood outside and scanned the crowd, asking anyone that passed by if they had extra tickets. I realized our chances were looking slim. This wasn't exactly the type of concert where you would find people scalping tickets. I felt somewhat embarrassed even asking anyone. Our friend Cathy had driven from Milwaukee to see the concert with us. So now we needed three tickets and couldn't find anyone who was selling even one. I tried convincing myself that if we were meant to be at this concert, we would be. As the crowd began to thin and the last few concertgoers made their way into the theatre, I looked up at the clouds and skeptically declared, "At this point, if we are going to go to this concert, the tickets are literally going to have to fall from the sky." A few moments later in a last half-hearted attempt, I approached a man who was walking down the street with a group of people and asked him if he had any tickets.

"How many do you need?" he asked, as he pulled out a stack of tickets.

"How much are you charging?" I asked, beaming with excitement.

"Nothing," he said. "They're free. I'm Mary Black's tour manager."

Patty had told me the night before she went back to Colorado, "If you want something in life, you have to ask for it."

She had changed a lot during the three months she was in Colorado. She was not just confident; she was glowing. Any traces of the "funk" I had been feeling during the winter months were suddenly forgotten. Patty was so alive. She was so self-assured and believed she was doing exactly what she was supposed be doing. Her enthusiasm was contagious.

The trials of starting a new life in Colorado had seemed to inspire Patty rather than discourage her. It wasn't because she had found the ultimate job or that everything had worked out perfectly. There were times of loneliness and doubt and some jobs she took that were not ideal. I remember her calling me crying once to say that she had spent her day cleaning toilets. Despite these challenges, she continued doing what she set out to do. As Patty described to me, she was living in one of the most beautiful places on earth and she met one amazing person after the next. Each day brought a new experience that allowed her to learn.

In my case, I was only looking for results. And as far as I was concerned, there were no results, just a process of trying to make "something" happen. I realize now that I simply panicked. I wanted something great to happen to prove that I was doing "something" worthwhile—or more to the point, that I was worthwhile. The moment I didn't get the results I was looking for, I doubted myself and the goals I was trying to accomplish. The purpose of our lives, I remembered, is not about what we achieve or that all our plans turn out the way we hoped. It's about what we experience while trying to make them happen. Through these trials, I felt like I was forced to learn that lesson all over again.

Patty reminded me of that lesson as I watched her light up when she talked about the new people she had met, the mountains she looked at every morning, and the new life she found the courage to live. Patty had accepted herself as a college-educated ski-lift ticket assistant and allowed herself to have the time of her life. She was living in the moment, realizing that every moment is a unique part of our path. As I saw it, it was Patty's ability to enjoy the ride that allowed her to feel a confidence that I'd never seen in her.

Inspired by this confidence, Patty convinced the owner of a whitewater rafting company to hire her for the summer as a tour guide. There were hundreds of applicants and limited positions. Even though Patty had never rafted before, she was determined to get the job. Not only had she never rafted before, I don't believe she had ever been camping. This job entailed both, all summer long. The owner explained to Patty that she was not experienced enough for this kind of job. Yet as Patty explained to me, she looked at him across the table and said, "I can do this job as well as anyone else and I will do whatever it takes to prove to you that I can."

Patty said she knew she was supposed to have the job. "You have to believe you can do anything you want to do. Don't take 'no' for an answer," she said, knowing it was a motto we both knew. Once again, I marveled at my friend's confidence and determination.

"What the hell have I been doing?" I thought to myself.

The answer was that I hadn't been asking for what I wanted—because I was afraid that what I really wanted might not work out. Lately, I was not practicing the act of not taking "no" for an answer. Listening to Patty, I was reminded that I hadn't always been a person who took "no" for an answer. Just four years earlier, Patty, our friend Adrienne, and I had traveled to Dublin, Ireland for two weeks the summer before our sophomore year in college. I was determined to accomplish what I came there to do. I was not leaving Ireland until I met the band U2. The year was 1989 and I was nineteen years old. I was also an aspiring singer and felt a profound affinity to this band and their music.

When Adrienne, Patty and I had first planned our trip, which was only a month before we arrived in Ireland, we had planned to visit Dublin, then make our way around the countryside from Cork to Kerry, to the Cliffs of Moher and other must-see destinations where some of Patty's relatives lived. Patty had a list of family members we planned to visit during our jam-packed itinerary. However, the day we arrived at the Shannon airport in Ireland, we didn't have a clue where to go next. Even though we discussed all the places we wanted to visit in Ireland before we left, we decided we'd wing it when we got there. Upon arrival and consumed with jetlag, we quickly decided we should take a four-hour train ride from Shannon to Dublin and start our trip from there. Patty promised to call her Aunt Annie, who lived in county Kerry, once we arrived in Dublin, so we could firm up our plans regarding our next destination. However, soon after we arrived in Dublin, and 20 hours of travel later, we discovered while riding in a taxi from the Dublin train station, that every hotel and hostel we tried finding a room at was booked. Unbeknownst to us, it was a bank holiday and the city was packed with tourists. Our kind-hearted taxi driver, who became our new best friend, told us about a place where there might be a room available. It was a small apartment complex called the Baggot Rath House, which was located on the outskirts of the city. Once we arrived, we discovered there was a temporary flat available, which included two bedrooms, a living room, a kitchen and a bathroom for a little cheaper per night than we'd pay at a hotel. We took it without hesitation. Suddenly we were "living" in an apartment in Dublin, Ireland.

The day we stepped foot in Dublin, we never left. We fell in love with the culture of the city, the music scene and the people we met. In a matter of days, we felt like locals and had the time of our lives being a part of it all. Despite Patty's best efforts of connecting with her relatives, it wasn't in the cards. Every day she would make a trip to the payphone to try to reach her Aunt Annie. However, Patty could never get through. Truthfully, as much as we all aspired to see all of Ireland, we could not pull ourselves away from Dublin. Personally, I was now at the epicenter of where I wanted to be and my dreams of meeting U2.

Of course, it wasn't as easy as that. We only had two weeks in Ireland. Despite all the people who we met who were either musicians, songwriters, artists, and locals who were a first cousin of someone who knew U2, my chances of meeting them seemed as slim as if I were in Chicago. I spent my days and nights telling myself that if it was supposed to happen it would. I also told myself that I would not give up no matter what. Alas, the second to our last night in Ireland, Adrienne and Patty and I met a lovely English gentleman named Owen, who wore a noticeably bright purple jacket with a rhinestone musical note pinned on his lapel, in a pub along the docks in the heart of

Dublin called Dockers. I have no idea what he was doing in Ireland nor did for a living, but we all enjoyed sharing some good banter over a few pints of Guinness together. About an hour into our conversation, Adrienne, Patty, and I were rehashing the amazing experiences we had during our trip, including our trip that very day to U2's rehearsal space at a place referred to as the "factory." A friend we had met in Dublin arranged for us to meet a musician friend of his at the factory, but it was a risky plan at best. Once we got in, we were on our own. Our visit to the factory didn't last long before we were politely escorted out, but nonetheless, it was a thrill to catch a glimpse of where the band rehearsed and knowing that we might see one of them at any given moment. I mentioned to Owen that as much as the three of us had come to Ireland to experience a trip abroad, I wanted nothing more than to meet U2. Even though we were leaving Ireland in two days, I still was hanging on to the hope that I would meet them. "I'm going to the factory tomorrow for business," Owen said. "You are welcome to join me."

I couldn't believe what he was saying…on the last night out of our trip no less. It was a dream come true. "Yes. I would love to," I said.

All I could focus on was the twinkle in the pin of his jacket that sparkled as we confirmed our plans to meet the next day. Even though I was utterly ecstatic, I tried to play it off as if I wasn't. After all, I had only known this guy for two hours and wasn't completely convinced that he might be full of crap or that he might kidnap me if given the chance. That was until another gentleman or bloke, who looked like he just returned from a punk rock tour, walked into the pub to meet Owen. As I soon found out, he happened to be one of the band's closest friends from grade school. He, too, planned to be at the factory the next day.

Soon after, Guggi, as he was named, arrived at the pub, Patty and Adrienne left to meet up with friends. I spent the rest of the evening walking the streets of Dublin with Owen and Guggi, trying to decipher all the cool things they were talking about through their thick accents, thinking that this was one of the coolest things I'd ever done in my life. We parted ways after grabbing a pint along our walk, and off I went, home to pray my heart out that this whole thing would indeed go down. Not only was there a full moon that night, there was an eclipse. Back at our flat, I sat staring into the face of the moon into the wee hours of the night. I'd never seen anything so magical in my life.

The next morning, I was in the canteen of the factory, which looked more like a grade school cafeteria, in a room filled with people including Bono, the Edge, Adam Clayton, and Larry Mullen Jr. sipping tea as I watched them all prepare for what seemed like a day of intense rehearsing. I mingled in as if I had business to do like everyone else. It was a day in the life, and so much more than I could have ever imagined. I sat there next to Owen, as he chatted away with the people he knew, sipping my tea just taking it all in.

That experience felt like a lifetime away as Patty and I sat on a bar stool at a place called Higgins Tavern in Wrigleyville. Patty was clearly in the zone of not taking "no" for an answer. Her spirit had evolved to a place where she was committed to making whatever happen she intended to do. The answer "no" means you keep asking again and again until you achieve what you want to achieve. Knowing what we want in life and remaining committed to our desires is the glory of the process. It's where the learning comes in. It is for us to know when we get there, that we truly belong.

I remember looking at Patty that night during our conversation and saying to myself, "Remember this."

The next day Patty planned to go to her mom's before going back to Colorado and I had plans to leave early in the morning to go to Lake Geneva. Even though we had already said our good-byes the night before, I decided to leave her a note on the bathroom mirror for when she woke up. In the back of my mind I thought somehow, by telling Patty to be careful on this next adventure, that she would be okay.

Dearest Patty,

I will see you soon. Be as careful as you can on those rivers. Please stay in one piece! I wish you the most wonderful days and experiences ahead. I will miss you and I love you! Thank you for a wonderful time, a compassionate ear, and just so much fun. Have a blast and be in touch soon. Your spirit has warmed my heart once again.

P.S. I didn't want to say goodbye again because it hurts my stomach!

I was happy to see when I returned home a note that Patty had left for me, as well.

Dearest Amy,

I will miss you again and again—it feels strange leaving again this time. I have a feeling of sadness. Thank you for making me feel so welcome and at home with you. I love that! I will call you soon. Hope Lake Geneva was beautiful.

P.S. I think I'm crying right now.

Love, Patty

If our lives are truly guided by a higher power and not by coincidence, then so many of our experiences make sense. Every experience made room for the next.

Coincidence is what I have come to know as divine purpose. Looking back, I almost feel like I could have seen it coming. Looking back, I finally understand the significance of so many of Patty's and my experiences.

I know why we experienced a spiritual awakening and a passion to understand, embrace and live it. I know why that experience allowed us to move beyond certain places in our lives that had been a struggle for a lifetime. I understand why so many of our conversations focused around the dynamics of change, loss, and creating our personal set of beliefs that inspired us to get through. I know why our friendship inspired us to seek a deeper level of awareness within ourselves, and why we both felt as equally in tune to each other. I understand why we had the times we shared in Lake Geneva and why we had to let it go. I know why we met the woman in Lake Geneva and Patty's subsequent encounter with Lynn. I can now see why something changed within each of us during our time in Colorado, and then inspired Patty to move there. I know why Patty wrote me such a profound letter in her journal, and why we promised each other that, whenever either of us saw a sunflower or a rose, we would know it was a sign of the other. More than anything, I understand why I was still in my apartment five days before Patty planned to be home again in Chicago, to receive her phone call.

Adrienne, my new roommate, stopped me as I was halfway out the door. "Wait, it's Patty," she said. For a second, I thought about telling Adrienne to ask Patty if I could call her back later that night. I quickly changed my mind when I realized Patty didn't have her own phone and how difficult it had been to get in touch with her.

"I'm so glad you caught me. I was already out the door. I've been trying to get in touch with you for days!" I said to Patty.

41

"It's really hard to get in touch here," she replied.

"How are you? Where are you?" I asked her.

"I'm okay," Patty said. I could hear from the tone of her voice that she wasn't.

"There has been a lot going on here," she continued to say.

Patty explained that a man who had been on their tour the week before had drowned while rafting. The river had been dangerously high that summer. Unfortunately, this man was not the first person who drowned while rafting over the summer. But it was the first time such a tragic accident happened during one of Patty's rides down the river. As she continued to explain, she and others had tried to give the man CPR, but were unsuccessful.

"I can't believe that happened. Why didn't you tell me sooner?" I asked her, stunned.

"I wanted to," she explained. "I didn't want it to sound like something that happened to me when it happened to him. I just needed to deal with it before I talked about it," Patty continued.

"Are you okay?" I asked her.

She said that she was, and that she had shared the experience with her mom. I was relieved to hear that her mom was helping her to deal with it.

We decided that we would continue our conversation when we saw each other on Sunday, when she planned to be home again. I could hear in Patty's voice that what happened on the river was still haunting her. There was so much I wanted to talk about, but we both decided we'd save it for when she got home, and we could talk in person. As we finished our conversation, we discussed whether Patty would need me to pick her up from the airport. We would talk on Friday morning to confirm any plans.

"I can't wait to see you and have endless time to reconnect," I said to her, as the tone of our conversation began to change in anticipation of Patty's arrival.

"I know, I can't wait either," she replied.

"Do you think we should go to…" I said, stopping myself in mid-sentence. "I know, I know, I'm late. We'll talk about it on Friday," even though I was feeling too excited to wait until Friday.

Patty laughed.

"Can't wait!" I told her.

"Me too," she said

"See you on Sunday!" I added.

I said goodbye, expecting to hear goodbye from her, too, as I went to hang up the phone.

"I love you," she replied, instead.

Since I was running late, my finger hit the receiver before I could respond, "I love you, too."

I thought for a minute about calling her back. I didn't have her number memorized, so I would have to find it. She knows I love her too, I thought to myself. I decided to tell her on Friday.

I believe in angels. I believe in energy, intuition, and miracles. Throughout our lives, we seek to understand these mysteries. In death, they are revealed. We are energetic, intuitive beings, and have the power to manifest miracles. We are here on this earthly plane to experience, to connect, to mend, to live out and to live within.

I had been sleeping so peacefully that Thursday night. Before falling asleep, I thought about Patty. I wondered if she would need me to pick her up from the airport like we discussed just two days earlier. We were so excited to see each other. She would be home from Colorado in three days and I could hardly wait. I started to imagine all the things we were going to do together and how impossible it would be to do everything in such a short amount of time. I wondered if Patty would be moving back to Chicago in October (as she had mentioned the last time we spoke). Perhaps she would continue with her new idea of river rafting in Costa Rica and maybe I would join her.

I thought about the last time that I saw Patty. Two months before, Michelle and I had taken a camping trip out west for ten days and made Colorado our last stop to visit Patty. When we arrived in Buena Vista, the town where Patty was living while she worked as a river guide, we had a hard time finding her. There wasn't one place in town where the river guides lived. After asking a few people who were hanging out at an abandoned gas station in the center of town, (who we soon found out were Patty's fellow guides and new dearest friends), we were told she could be anywhere from the middle of a nearby mountain where she camped or hanging out with friends in one of their "Barney's," which was a van or bus that many of the river guides used as a makeshift home. Michelle and I were out of our element. After spending more time than we were used to roughing it out in the wilderness, we were longing for the comforts of home. By the time we found Patty, which was late into the night, as excited as we were to finally see each other, we were all totally exhausted and needed to get some sleep.

The next morning Patty left on the 7:00 a.m. river trip with her crew and returned later that day to take Michelle and me on the afternoon ride. It was an amazing experience to raft down the Arkansas River with Patty as our guide and experience the life she had come to love. However, it didn't leave much downtime in our day. When we returned from rafting, Michelle and I had to prepare to make the three-hour journey to Boulder to see my brother before starting our drive back to Chicago the following day. Even in the short amount of time we had together, it seemed like nothing had changed. Patty and I laughed together as we always had and simply enjoyed the comfort of being in each other's presence. Throughout that afternoon, we kept saying to each other, "I wish we had more time."

When it was finally time for Michelle and I to leave, I felt a pit in the bottom of my stomach. As Michelle waited for me in our car, Patty and I sat in the front seat of her car and said our good-byes. "It's funny sitting here again. I feel like we're supposed to go somewhere," I told her.

"It is strange," Patty replied. "I feel like that too."

As we continued to talk, Patty took a big sip of her water bottle. Just as I always tried to do, I said something to make her laugh, so I could watch her spit out her water. It was good hearing her laugh with me again. Even though we ended our conversation in such a good and familiar way, I felt a lump in my throat as we finally hugged and said good-bye.

Thinking back on that night, I was so relieved to know that Patty would be back in Chicago soon. Even though it had only been two months since we were together in Colorado, it felt like so much time had passed. I could hardly wait to talk again in person. I also couldn't wait to discuss how painful it felt as we said our goodbyes the last time we saw each other. There was something about that experience that haunted me. Every time I thought about it my eyes welled up with tears. I assured myself that the memory of that sadness would soon be forgotten.

As I let that thought go, I stared out my bedroom window and watched white puffy clouds sail across the night sky. It was a beautiful sight. I was struck by their presence. I couldn't help but think there was a special meaning hidden behind them. "God," I whispered softly to myself, contemplating His mystery. "Maybe He was close," I thought. "God, God, God," I whispered as I fell asleep.

Somewhere in my dreams that night, I found myself sitting on a picnic bench in the middle of a huge valley surrounded by the most beautiful mountains. The sun was setting behind my back. There was a person sitting across from me and we were holding each other's hands. Although I couldn't see the person's face, I felt a strong connection to them. I also knew that when the sun set this person was going to die.

It didn't feel like death as I had known it to be. As I understood it, this person was moving on to a place that neither of us had ever experienced before. Wherever it was they were going, I knew I would not see them again. There were no words spoken between us. We both intuitively knew that we were supposed to be with each other through this experience. Even though we both sat there calmly, I could feel my heart pounding. As we sat together holding hands, I kept looking over my shoulder anxiously waiting for the sun to set.

In the next scene of my dream, I was in a funeral home attending someone's wake. Again, I couldn't see the person's face. But I knew it was the person I was with in the valley. The next thing I knew, someone had their arm around me and was trying to comfort me. I was overwhelmed with grief as different people gathered around me and began expressing their condolences for my loss. I woke up abruptly to that image, not sure of reality. My whole body was shaking. I reassured myself several times that it was just a bad dream. The first thing that morning, I called my mom to confirm that nothing bad had happened and that my experience the night before was only just a dream.

Later that day, I was in the suburbs where my parents lived to pick up my car that was being repaired. As I walked into my family's kitchen, laughing with my sister, my mom interrupted us and said she had awful news to share. She followed close behind me as I went to set my things down. I felt butterflies in my stomach. "What happened?" I asked.

"Something awful," she said looking straight at me.

"Bad,?" I replied hoping to lessen any exaggeration to this news.

"Horrible," she said as tears welled in her eyes.

My heart was in my throat. "Patty?" I whispered, not wanting to know.

"Yes," she nodded.

"Dead,?" I asked, sick to hear the answer.

"Yes," she said.

I stood frozen in disbelief as my mom explained what happened. The night before, Patty was in a car accident. It happened on a two-lane highway in the middle of a desolate valley in Colorado. She was alone as she drove from her home in Breckenridge to Buena Vista, where she would see her river rafting friends before leaving for Chicago the following Sunday. Just 10 miles short of her destination, her car veered over the far-right side of the road. Apparently, she hit a small boulder that was tucked within the grass on the shoulder. Patty's car flipped several times and she was killed instantly.

In that instant, one million thoughts raced through my mind. I pictured Patty driving along, unaware of what was about to happen to her. How did she not survive this? How could she, at 24 years of age, no longer be alive? It was not real. Thoughts of Patty's mom and brother came to my mind. "They cannot know this," I thought. I could not fathom them walking around with this news in their hearts. I was overwhelmed thinking of what their pain must be as my own shock consumed me.

I walked around my house aimlessly as I tried coping with emotions I'd never felt before. "This is not happening, this is not happening," I sobbed. I went outside for a moment to try to calm myself down. As I stood alone in my front yard, I looked over my shoulder and noticed that I was standing next to one single sunflower that was taller than I. It startled me. I wondered where the sunflower had come from. Standing next to it felt comforting. However, its calming affect was soon overshadowed by the deepest pain I had ever felt.

I felt the pain of so many losses all at once. I felt the loss of the wonderful person I knew. I felt the end of Patty's and my friendship and the end of knowing anything familiar at all. I felt lost. I needed something to grasp onto. I wondered, "How am I going to get through this?" I wasn't sure how I was going to walk the 10 steps it would take to get back into my house, let alone how I would heal from one of the deepest losses I had ever felt. How was I going to get through this without Patty?

I couldn't believe it when I "felt" an answer. Something told me that I would have to learn to connect with Patty on a totally different level. I recalled the previous months when Patty was in Colorado and we would say to each other, "I'm with you. I'm with you in spirit." This belief had always been a comforting and easy one to accept. Now I was forced to live it.

The next 24 hours felt like a lifetime of pain as I anxiously awaited the arrival of my friends who were rushing to get into town. Everyone finally arrived and gathered at my apartment. We spent the evening planning Patty's eulogy to give at her funeral. All of us, including Patty's brother John, spent hours reminiscing at the "round table" as Patty and I called it, in the dining room of our apartment.

Beyond the sadness, an indescribable energy filled the room that was felt by all of us. It was an energy that radiated joy, love, peace, laughter and everything to us that was Patty. We felt the blessing Patty's life was to ours, knowing it would be each of our own journeys as we continued to know it in our lives. Suddenly I remembered our pact when we promised each other that, whenever either of us saw a sunflower or a rose, we would know it was a "sign" of the other. Finally, I realized the significance of that conversation. I was speechless as I thought of my experience the day before, standing in my front yard just moments after I learned the news of Patty's death. I was in the company of a sunflower.

As each of us shared countless stories about Patty that night, together we felt an overwhelming sense of her presence. For us, it felt like Patty was just as much a part of our conversation as any of us who were there. That night all of us revealed how close we felt to Patty even though she was gone. As I looked at my friends sitting around the table, I was overwhelmed with gratefulness. On a night that was otherwise tragic, we created the blueprint for healing. We allowed ourselves in that evening to feel the spirit of Patty's presence even though physically she was no longer there.

Unfortunately, we cannot always live in a state of those sustaining moments. In the days that followed, Patty's family and friends went through some of the hardest and saddest moments of our lives. After the funeral services in Chicago, Patty's mom (so generously) invited me to accompany her and Patty's brother John to Colorado for a memorial service in honor of Patty. Patty's friends in Colorado had planned a special service that would take place alongside the Arkansas River, which Patty had come to love so much. During this time, we would also collect Patty's things and visit the site of the car accident. I felt so honored by the invitation and eagerly and gratefully accepted. Somewhere in my heart I believed that in Colorado I would see Patty again.

Patty's mom, brother John, and I arrived in Colorado to the most beautiful fluorescent blue sky that I had ever seen. The beauty was almost painful. I had never felt so vulnerable in all my life. Everything at that moment seemed to hurt. Our plan was to drive straight from the airport to Patty's home in Breckenridge where she had lived with two other roommates. As we made our way there, even the enormous scene of the Rocky Mountains couldn't distract us from how painstakingly difficult it was to take this journey.

After a long car ride of feeling both eagerness and anxiety about seeing Patty's home, we finally arrived at her house in Breckenridge. I hoped that I would feel a sense of comfort by being there. However, the moment we walked through the door, the only thing I felt was her absence. We met her roommates and took our time just looking around the house and her bedroom. Everything was just as she had left it. We began going through her things trying to decide what we should keep and what to give away. We quickly realized that there was more to do, both physically and emotionally, than we were prepared to do. Ultimately, we decided it would be best to wait until the morning to finish packing Patty's things.

That night, Patty's roommates invited me to stay at their house, which I was happy to do. I decided to sleep in Patty's room. I thought that by staying in her room I would feel closer to her. Somewhere in the back of my mind, I thought Patty was going to come waltzing into the room with a big smile on her face, just like she always did. With every minute that passed, it became painfully clear that this wasn't going to happen.

Not only was Patty gone, every attempt I tried to physically connect with her, whether it was by sleeping in her room or being near her things, just led me deeper into my loss.

Somewhere around midnight that night, unable to sleep, I sat in Patty's bed staring out the window into the night sky where a million stars hung underneath it. The only thing I could hear was silence. I wondered if I was going to make it through the night without losing my mind. I had never felt so alone. I desperately wanted to know that Patty and I were still connected. I wanted to know that we could still communicate. I wanted to know that she was with me as I was going through one of the most painful experiences of my life.

Staring around her room in thought, I found myself gazing at a picture that hung above Patty's bed. Suddenly a burst of reality shot into focus. I grabbed the picture off the wall and held it to my chest in tears. Sitting in a frame was the card that Patty's friend Bob had shared with us the previous New Year's Eve. To read these words now and on this night, all I could think about was how much I wanted to hold them close to my heart forever. They were words I could hear Patty saying to me now.

Home is where I want to be. Pick me up and turn me 'round. I feel numb, born with a weak heart. So I guess I must be having fun. The less we say about it the better. Make it up as we go along. Feet on the ground, head in the sky, It's O.K... I know nothing's wrong.

I got plenty of time; you got light in your eyes.

And you're standing here beside me. I love the passing of time. Never for money, always for love. Cover up and say goodnight, say goodnight.

Home is where I want to be, but I guess I'm already there.

I come home. She lifted up her wings. Guess this must be the place.

I can't tell one from another. Did I find you, or you find me? There was a time

before we were born, if someone asks, this is where I'll be.

We drift in and out. Sing into my mouth.

Out of all those kinds of people, you've got a face with a view.

And I am just an animal looking for a home. Share the same space for a

minute or two.

And you love me until my heart stops; love me until I'm dead.

Eyes that light up. Eyes look through you.

Cover up the blank spots. Hit me on the head.

Say goodnight, say goodnight.

The next morning Patty's mom, brother, and I gathered together to begin what we came to do in Colorado. We spent the morning packing Patty's room. Next, we visited the river rafting company where she worked that summer. Meeting Patty's friends, the people she worked with, and seeing the places where she spent her time felt surreal without Patty. Everyone we spoke with told us how they loved her and had so many stories to share about Patty, even after only knowing her a few months. I wasn't surprised to hear this, which made me miss her even more.

Later that day, the three of us left Breckenridge and made our way to Buena Vista, the town where Patty had worked and lived that summer, near the scene of the accident. We took the same drive that Patty did from Breckenridge to Buena Vista, looking for the highway marker to find the exact site of the accident. When we found the site, it was hard to imagine how it happened. There were no treacherous mountain curves like the one we had just driven from. Patty was driving along a two-lane highway in the middle of a valley and, for some unknown reason, her car veered off the right side of the road. There was a dip in the middle of the shoulder where a small boulder was tucked within the grass. Patty's car hit the boulder and she lost control of the car.

Patty's mom, brother, and I walked the path where the car flipped and picked up the debris that flew out of the car window while we carefully pieced together how the accident happened. As we walked this path, we discovered that the side of the road was flat just a few yards further where the accident occurred. The three of us stood in silence as we realized what might have been if only Patty would have made it a few more yards ahead.

Next, we drove to the place where Patty's car was being held, which was at a parking lot behind a truck stop in town. We wanted to see the car for ourselves and salvage what we could from her belongings. It was a devastating sight to see her car. The moment we saw it, the impact of the accident became clear. The reality of it all hit hard again. It was difficult to believe that something like this could happen to someone we loved so much.

Patty's mom, John, and I quickly went through Patty's car as we tried to decide what to leave behind and what to take with us. The car was filled with luggage that was not only packed for her trip home to Chicago, but for a trip to Ireland that she and her family had planned to take. Since Patty was living between Breckenridge and Buena Vista that summer, the trunk of her car looked like an open dresser drawer. I laughed to myself at the Patty I knew.

The only personal item I hoped to salvage was Patty's journal—the same journal I

54

gave to her to use for our collaborated "book." Since she had shared what she wrote with me openly the last time she was home, I felt determined to find it. At last, as the three of us painfully tried to retrieve what we could from her car, we found the journal. In that moment, I held on to it for dear life, thinking of how meaningful the thoughts Patty shared in her journal would now be.

After seeing the accident site and going through Patty's car, I wanted to curl up in a ball and go home. I wished so much that I could share these experiences with my friends in Chicago. Patty knew and was close to many different groups of people from Chicago to Colorado, all of whom were experiencing a very deep loss. Since I didn't know her friends in Colorado and I was not a family member, I had only myself to commiserate with.

I wanted to be strong and support Patty's mom and brother John, so I did my best not to appear like the basket case I felt like inside. At times throughout our journey, I felt like I could have cried morning, noon, and night and it still wouldn't be enough to make the pain go away. Grief wasn't an emotion but an enormous physical pain that I had never experienced before. I still had not come to grips with the fact that I had to go through it without Patty.

I recalled the year before when a young woman that Patty and I knew died in a drowning accident. Just two weeks before she drowned, we met Liz at Chuck's in Lake Geneva. Patty, Liz and I were introduced by a mutual friend, and the three of us fell into instant conversation. When Patty and I heard about Liz's accident, we were both shaken by the news. It was hard to believe that this young and vibrant woman was gone.

As fate would have it, we discovered that Patty's boyfriend grew up with Liz and that they were close friends. Therefore, he asked Patty to accompany him to Liz's wake. At first, this wasn't something Patty thought she could do. Ever since her father died, she had a difficult time making it through any kind of situation that reminded her of that experience. Patty knew the indescribable loss that Liz's family and friends were going through. She also realized that the pain of her dad's sudden death was still very real for her.

Patty and I spent many hours talking about this and how much she wanted to move on from reliving that experience. She knew the service for Liz was about someone else's loss and not her own. It was a cathartic experience for Patty and she believed there was a reason she was faced with it. Before she left for the service, I gave her a small pep talk and reminded her to be strong. Now I was the one who desperately needed Patty's support and comfort. I found myself saying to her, "Can you believe this is happening? I cannot believe this is happening to us!"

Patty's family and I had one more task to perform before her memorial service that evening. Patty's tent still needed to be packed up and taken down. She had set up her tent on a beautiful spot in the middle of a small mountain overlooking the Arkansas River. Whenever I would try to picture it from Patty's description, I could never imagine it. Not until Michelle and I visited her two months before, the three of us sleeping side by side, could I believe this was her home. I was shocked that Patty wasn't scared out of her mind living in a tent alone in the middle of a mountain! However, it was only after seeing the breathtaking view Patty woke up to every morning that I began to understand.

Patty's memorial service began at 7:00 p.m. Patty's mom, brother John, and I arrived together shortly before it began and spent time getting to know more of Patty's friends from Colorado. Everyone gathered under a picnic pavilion where the service was being held, which was just a few feet away from the river where Patty rafted that summer. Although it was a warm summer evening, there was a strong wind that was becoming a nuisance. As a matter of fact, while people were setting up for her service, the flowers, candles, and poster-size pictures of Patty rafting down the river kept falling off the tables. It was nearly impossible to light any of the candles. Several of us worked to keep the candles lit and everything on the table had to be held down.

The service began with the song "The Rose." I wondered if it was just a coincidence or if her friends knew how much Patty loved this song. An even greater coincidence, however, was that by the middle of the song, the wind had virtually disappeared.

The next thing I knew, as people took turns sharing their stories and tribute to Patty, there was total stillness. The candles stayed lit and the flowers and pictures displayed on the picnic tables stood still. I had never experienced such a phenomenon. Patty must be trying to get our attention, I thought to myself. It seemed so obvious that I wanted to stand up and say, "Am I hallucinating or is anyone else noticing this?"

Although I was moved by the powers that be, the sadness of Patty's death was overwhelming. After everything that Patty's family and I had gone through during the last three days, let alone the last week, I felt like I was cracking. It finally hit me. It was too much to take. In that moment, my heart could not grieve anymore.

As the service came to an end, Patty's friends asked everyone to join them in one final ritual. They carved her name with a small heart inscribed next to it into a small log of a tree, which they planned to send down the river. Followed by all of us who attended the service, Patty's brother John did the honor of carrying the log to the edge of the water. Standing before the sunset, we stood around him as he gently released this symbol of our love for Patty into the mouth of the river. As I watched the body of this tree float away, I felt as though it took a part of all our hearts with it. Mine ached so badly.

After the service, everyone stood together talking and comforting each other. I walked away from the group to take a moment away from it all. As I walked, I prayed and asked, and pleaded all at once for a moment of relief. I then found my walk had led me further alongside the river and in front of a Colorado sky that stopped me in my tracks. I stood still and breathed in its peace.

As I stood gazing into this amazing scene, I found myself talking to Patty as if she were listening. I told her how difficult this experience was and that I needed a break from the pain. Immediately I felt as though I heard her say, "Of course you do!" It wasn't the words that felt familiar but the energy I felt when I heard them. Suddenly I recalled the spiritual lessons I had learned through of our friendship. I knew then we would always be connected in spirit. The energy between us would never die. For the past several days, I had been desperately searching for a sign of Patty. At that moment, I felt her right beside me.

I wanted to hold on to that moment forever. For the first time since Patty's death I felt a sense of hope. I understood our friendship had taken a new turn. Just as we told each other before Patty left for Colorado, "We are taking our friendship to the next level." As I stood looking at the sunlit mountains, I knew something amazing would come from this experience. I was grateful for the journey I saw before me. "Thank you," I whispered. "Thank you."

I wanted to take a picture to remember the moment. It was 7:45 p.m., which was about the same time and exactly one week to the day that Patty died. Standing before the sunset, I took a picture to remember … that in spirit our friendship would always live.

By the time I got home, I had three rolls of film from Colorado to be developed. I tried to take as many pictures as possible so our friends at home could see every part of the experience. I felt as though my days in Colorado were an out of body experience. I looked forward to seeing the photos myself.

I went to pick up my film a few days later and had forgotten about the picture I had taken at the memorial service. It was just one of many. As I paid for my film, I wondered if perhaps I would notice a little bird or rainbow or something that only I would know was a sign from Patty. While Patty's family and I were in Colorado, we constantly took notice of things that might be a sign of Patty's "presence," like clusters of white oversized clouds that reflected colors of the rainbow, or definite rays of the sun that colored the sky. It was a moment of vulnerability that allowed us to be open to the gift of seeing things, which in our everyday lives we are never vulnerable enough to see.

Since there were three packs of photos to go through, I reminded myself to keep an open eye. The very first picture I saw took my breath away. It was the picture I had taken at the memorial service.

I couldn't believe what I was seeing as I stared into this white, angelic figure with wide-open wings—the picture on the cover this book. Instantly I knew it was Patty. I don't know how many times I repeated the words, "Oh my God!" However, the next thought I spoke aloud was, "I knew it!"

Staring into my picture I felt as if I could hear Patty saying, "I am here! I am here!

I am in, and connected to, the light."

I responded, "I see you Pat, I really do. You are an angel, a reflection of everything we learned through our friendship, and I knew that I would see you again."

The angelic figure I saw in my picture proved to me that everything Patty and I learned on a spiritual level during our friendship was true. For me, it couldn't feel any more real than this. I couldn't believe that the energy of our spirits would cease because our bodies did. It is when I look at this picture that I am reminded of the words that Patty and I would often say to one another, "I am so amazed, but not surprised."

I kept reminding myself after Patty died to "be open." It was the catchphrase that Patty and I came to apply to so many situations. Being open to perceive, experience and know something different taught me time and time again that miracles can happen when your heart is open. Even though circumstances in my life had changed, this principle would not. We must be open to miracles if we want to experience them. I realized that if my heart wasn't open, even when I wanted to retreat into a pain that felt hopeless, my picture would not exist.

Patty and I spent the last two years of our friendship discovering this lesson. Learning to be open is what helped us to grow by leaps and bounds. It is a lesson that opened the door to so many other lessons. Being open to the idea that life will change for the better during difficult times is challenging. The result, as Patty and I would discuss, was worth any challenge. That was the beauty of it. So many of the painful experiences we struggled to move beyond, we saw change in an instant. Those were the times that held me in awe of the wisdom of the Universe, God, and life.

Shortly after Patty died, I went with my brother to a local bar that was one of Patty's and my favorite hangouts. During that time, I was so aware of my sadness. I could feel it from the time I woke up in the morning and through every moment of the day as I tried living my life again. I was sad, yet at the same time, I was desperately trying to find my way out of it. Inspired by the angel I saw in my picture, I believed that I would.

I thought that by going somewhere familiar I might feel more like myself again.

Shortly after my brother and I arrived, I played some songs on the jukebox for nostalgia's sake. Unfortunately, I soon realized that trying to indulge in the good old days seemed to magnify their absence. I stood looking around at this once familiar place and realized now that nothing felt familiar at all.

I took a seat at the bar and patiently waited for something to happen that would bring me back to a time when everything was good, I was happy, and Patty was alive. I wanted to be 23 years old again, hovering around the pool table, and like every other person I observed that night who was laughing along with their best friend. I wanted to know that Patty was with me. I refused to believe that I was doomed to feel a sense loss beyond measure. I wanted to see things differently—I was determined to be open.

As I sat wrestling with both pain and faith, side by side, I noticed a poster on the wall with an Old Irish proverb that read, "May the road rise to meet you, May the wind be always at your back. May the sunshine warm upon your face, and the rain fall soft upon your fields. And until we meet again, may God hold you."

Patty was always in the spirit of being Irish, and the Irish who met her always loved her. She would sing to me the traditional Irish folksongs that her father had sung to her, always in a melodramatic way. Cherishing those memories, I thought about all the times that I had randomly glanced at this poster. This time, though, I was overwhelmed as I sat silently honoring Patty through this blessing of farewell.

Earlier in the evening, my brother had asked me if I would like to be his partner in a game of pool. Since playing pool was one of Patty's and my favorite things to do together, I eagerly accepted. I could finally connect to a time when I felt like myself. I could feel what it was like again when Patty and I would play pool for hours, feeling as, "on" as Patty and I would say with the night as our pool game.

Despite my intentions, I was playing horribly. I was disappointed to say the least. It wasn't that I necessarily cared about winning a pool game, as much as I wanted to know Patty was with me. If I could just hit one ball on the table, then I could prove to myself that she was here. As I aligned the cue behind the ball (in the same focused and self-assured way that Patty and I used to whenever we played), I thought for sure that Patty was going to miraculously help me make my chosen shot. Just then, I sank the eight ball and lost the game. With that, I couldn't help but laugh at myself. I went outside to get some air knowing that it was time to get a grip.

I walked around a bit to clear my thoughts and concluded that I should not rest my hopes of knowing happiness based on a pool game. I also realized the more I tried to recognize a sign from Patty, the more alone I felt. Standing outside, these thoughts continued to reel through my head. I made a conscious choice to let them go. Suddenly it struck me what I needed to do: I needed to be open. I had to stop trying to relive the past. I needed to be open to the present moment. I knew that a sign would come when my heart was open to see it.

"Now what?" I wondered.

"Pray. Pray for a miracle," something told me. So I did.

I took a breath and went back inside, telling myself that I was going to try this night again. I also decided that I would take another crack at playing pool. This time however, I would not be playing with the same expectations. I would be open to whatever that meant. Suddenly the lesson of being open seemed so much bigger. It is the spiritual act, of letting go.

A few moments later I noticed three college-aged girls who all happened to be wearing bright orange sweatshirts. I took note of their friendship and the constant laughter they were sharing. We exchanged smiles as I couldn't help but think about the way it feels to be surrounded by your circle of friends.

As my brother and I continued our game, I felt more and more in touch with a familiar part of myself. (At the same time, I also happened to be playing pool better than ever.) For the first time since Patty died, I saw the sadness I felt as something that was to be expected, rather than something that I failed to overcome. Because Patty blessed me with the gift of my amazing picture, I felt that I should be stronger. I wanted to be stronger. I had to stop blaming myself for what I was feeling. It wasn't strength that I was lacking, I realized, it was surrender.

Discovering such realizations is what inspired Patty and me to share in endless conversations at our kitchen table. I could almost see the two of us sitting across from each other as we would describe the intricate details of every experience we went through. Patty and I connected on such a powerful level because of the way we supported each other as we processed the lessons we were learning. "It's about growth," we had always said. Tonight, it suddenly seemed like nothing had changed.

I had been looking for a sign of Patty all throughout the night. The moment I let go, I felt Patty's presence in a way that seemed so alive. I suddenly recognized a part of myself again. I realized then that living with an open heart was the only way our friendship could live. That would mean being open to the present moment, accepting what is, and remembering that life gives us in return what we choose to let go. Patty's death made living those spiritual lessons that much harder.

Suddenly I heard the words, "Be open. Be open to feel, to grieve, to heal and you will." I felt a sense of relief come over me. Regardless of what came next, I believed I was given the answer of what I needed to do.

My brother and I continued with our pool game and we chatted with the three girls in the orange sweatshirts in between games. After sharing some initial small talk, I asked them why they were all wearing orange sweatshirts. They laughed and joked about what they must look like dressed in such a way, and told me about the wonderful weekend they had just spent at one of their family's summer cottages. Just for fun and because they were all best friends, they decided to buy the same color sweatshirts they found in a local shop. I enjoyed listening to their story and we felt an instant connection because that was something the girls and I would have done.

We continued talking and began exchanging our own experiences of what it means to be a part of a sacred group of friends. I told them about Allison, Cathy, Dara, Michelle and Patty and our own "girls weekends," and what those times meant to us. These young women were all ears as I continued to tell them more about my friendships with the girls and the bond that had grown between us. For a moment, I thought about telling them about Patty and some of the life changing experiences we shared, but I wasn't sure if I should take the conversation down that road. But the girls were so enthusiastic, and kept asking me more questions that I decided to share some of my favorite Patty stories with them, which included the countless times that Patty and I would find ourselves on any random night in deep conversation with people we just met!

Maybe it was just because we were all in the moment, but as the girls and I continued to talk, our conversation grew more and more intense. "What happened next?

Where is Patty now?" they wanted to know eagerly.

Since the focus of our conversation felt so positive, I didn't want to tell them that Patty had died. But I quickly realized that Patty's death was the reason we were even having this conversation! At that point, I knew without a doubt that there was a reason these girls and I had met, and I knew they were supposed to hear the whole story.

By the time I went through the story of the sunflower and the rose, Patty's death, my angel picture, and the fact that I knew that Patty's and my friendship would continue to live, we all were in tears. But they weren't tears of sadness as much as they were tears of feeling so moved by the story I had just shared with them. I was overwhelmed with happiness. In that moment, the story of Patty's and my friendship felt so alive.

"I feel Patty!" one of the girls exclaimed.

There was a feeling of Patty's spirit that was obvious to all of us. It felt as real as if Patty and I were standing side by side. Because of the enthusiasm, energy and connection that the girls and I shared, I knew Patty was there. It was a true Patty moment.

I couldn't help but think that what I had just experienced was nothing short of a miracle. I remembered that I had prayed for one. In that moment, I knew for the rest of my life to believe in miracles. I remembered it was during my friendship with Patty that I first came to know the meaning of a miracle. I knew in my heart that I had just experienced one.

The girls and I were all talking excitedly at once and in awe, about what we as strangers had just shared. We all hugged and said our goodbyes.

"Thank you so much!" I said.

"No, thank you. That was totally amazing!" they all said at once.

We finished our conversation, realizing there was nothing more that could be said. The energy that surrounded us could not be described in words. As I left the bar and walked toward my car, I turned back to see the three of them hanging their heads out the door, waving and shouting goodbye.

"I can't believe that just happened," I said to myself, feeling so elated as I got in my car.

As soon as I turned on the radio, the song that was playing confirmed the experience I just went through: "Surrender, let it go. If I could, I would, set your spirit free."

"It's not something good, it's not something bad, but things will never be the same." I asked Patty to write that down on a napkin we found in the glove compartment of our car during one of our fall Sunday afternoon drives. We would record it later in the "log" we were keeping. I didn't know what it was supposed to mean at the time. It just came to me and it felt right to write it down. So many things were changing, as they should when you're 24 years old. Life always changes. To realize that it's not good or bad—that it is just change—is something more to swallow. "What is meant to be will be, and that is the purpose of every moment," Patty and I both agreed as we learned life's way.

I found that napkin crumpled up in an old journal the following October, three months after Patty died. The significance of those words overwhelmed me. We had written those words one year earlier. It was a day we felt confident to take on life's changes. Now, I found myself challenged to grasp them again. I wondered to myself whether Patty and I somehow knew that something was about to change dramatically.

Death is one of the most difficult changes to accept. For me, it felt as though my body had fallen away from my soul. There is an overwhelming sense of grief when you realize a person you love is no longer of this world. The world feels a little different, a little less. Not only does the world as we know it change, but there is a part of ourselves that seems a little less. We grieve for the person who died, and we must grieve for the person in ourselves whom we once knew. It's more than an impression on our lives. It changes who we are.

I am no longer the same. I miss Patty and I miss the person I was before she died. It's a daily act of acceptance. It is a challenge to not focus on the past, of what used to be. I had to trust that I would feel good again, trust that there would be happiness, and that I would be able to accept what had changed within me. When I think of Patty, I remember how she thought I was as special to her as she was to me. I would have to live in that light again. I would have to love life again.

If we are open and grateful when someone comes into our life, we must also be open and grateful when someone must go. As a friend of mine so beautifully shared with me, "If someone you cared about was leaving to a place that was right for them, would you ever say, 'Don't go, stay here for me?' And if you asked them to stay and they did, denying where they needed to be, would the relationship be free? Would it be true?"

I learned through my friendship with Patty that people are gifts to us. No one person can ever offer the same experience as another. At times, I find myself searching to find another person or experience that could replace that void. Still, I know it will never be the same and I have learned that it's not supposed to be.

Mother Teresa said that those who are near death know that God is close. If it is true that we leave this life when we have fulfilled the purpose God has for us, I feel blessed to have shared so closely the last three years of Patty's life with her. Before Patty moved to Colorado, we promised each other that we would continue to live all that we learned through our friendship. We learned to accept change and grow with it. In retrospect, I realize it wasn't just Patty's venture to Colorado we were preparing ourselves for. Through our friendship, we shared with each other the lessons that one of us needed to die and the other would need to live.

On my 24th birthday, the last birthday I ever celebrated with Patty at my house in Lake Geneva, she gave me a gift of an anonymous poem called *Look to this Day*. It was a poem that Patty's father had passed on to her. They became words of inspiration I would need to live by for the rest of my life. They were words that both Patty and I had finally come to understand. As Patty stated in her journal, "Thank you dad, for teaching me such wonderful words."

Look to this day, for it is life ...

The very life of life.

In its brief course

Lies all the realities and verities of existence ...

The bliss of hope,

The splendor of action,

The glory of power.

For yesterday was but a dream,

And ... tomorrow is only a vision,

But, today... well lived ...

Makes every yesterday a dream of happiness,

And every tomorrow a vision of hope...

.... One day at a time.

Things do change. Patty and I once shared these words that I would now need to accept—words that set the tone for what it means to experience a spiritual lesson. Just as we had supported each other through our friendship, I knew Patty would be with me in spirit as I learned to accept this change of life. I realized that there would always be sadness in my heart that Patty was no longer here in the way she used to be. I also realized that, over time, I would know peace again. Only opening my heart to the good in life would tell.

I now know why "Bittersweet" was one of Patty's favorite songs. I know why it was her favorite request every time my brother would play guitar for us. It was for each of us who were struggling with this change to remember that with the bad also comes the good. The mystery, the lessons learned, and the gifts that come from accepting both the good and bad, is the power behind the word "bittersweet." It is always when I remember this lesson that I will happen to hear a song like that one, and know that somewhere Patty is singing loudly with me.

Again, as I focused on the meaning of those words on that crumpled napkin, I realized it all comes down to, "It's not something good, it's not something bad, but things will never be the same." It is the meaning of change, a simple word that sparks the fear of death itself within us. I know living is not about staying stuck in the good or the bad. Life is about living the experiences your spirit has come here to live.

Patty left behind something I will never forget—a picture that symbolizes even more than what it appears to be. Through this picture, I will always see in it life's beauty, meaning, and a reflection of one of the most amazing experiences of my life. But even more than that, I will always remember the spirit I have become by learning to accept what can never be the same.

I feel the times that Patty is with me. I know that I can always find her in my heart. However, I've discovered the only way to do this is to let her go. In spirit, there is no need to hold on. Grief has taught me that letting go of wanting things or people to be the way you want them to be is what releases you from pain. To let someone go says to them, "I respect who you are and your path of life." It's an act of love.

On the first anniversary of Patty's death, Allison, Cathy, Dara, Michelle and I decided to go to Lake Geneva. We spent the day just hanging out together and found ourselves going back and forth between moments of sadness and laughter. We took turns sharing our favorite Patty stories. We also took turns sharing our own accounts, as we had done so many times that year, when we first learned the news that Patty had died.

I couldn't believe that an entire year had passed. It felt like I had anticipated the first anniversary of Patty's death all year long. It was a year that seemed one of the hardest of my life. That year was a series of "firsts" for everything: the first birthday, the first Christmas, and any day that Patty was no longer there as she was the year before. Maybe now I could stop looking at everything as the sting of her death all over again. In a way, I hoped it would be a new beginning for myself.

That night the girls and I planned to go to a friend's annual summer farm party. A good friend of Patty's and mine would also be there playing with his band. Being outside on a warm summer night, surrounded with great music, with all of us together seemed like the perfect thing to do. It was the kind of night that Patty would have loved. Even though I was unsure whether I was in a socializing mood, I could almost hear Patty saying in the exact way that she would, "Absolutely, you should go!"

The party was held in a wide-open field surrounded by the landscape of open farmland bordering Wisconsin's country roads. The girls and I made our way around the party having fun as we usually did. It was a trait that I loved about us. Being together in this way was exactly what all of us needed.

As we waited for the band to start, the five of us gathered near the front of the stage. Even though all of us had put forth our best efforts to enjoy the moment, I couldn't stop looking at my watch waiting for 7:45 p.m. to arrive, the time Patty died. The significance of this time felt too meaningful to forget. I was also preoccupied by the fact that the sky was still grey when the one thing I wanted was to see a glimpse of the sun.

Patty loved sunsets. I often thought how symbolic it was that she died at the time of sunset. I thought about the dream I had the night Patty died, where I was holding someone's hand as we waited for the sun to set. The picture I had taken at Patty's memorial service was taken at sunset because I wanted to remember what the last sunset Patty might have seen looked like. "Where is the sunset now?" I wondered.

I was certain that we would see a sunset in memory of Patty's anniversary. To me it would prove that she was every bit a part of this experience. Throughout the past year, I had received so many signs from Patty. Tonight, more than ever, I wanted to see one again. Every moment that passed by, it became more evident that we wouldn't see a sunset. At that moment, I missed Patty so much.

"It's okay," I said trying to comfort myself. "If I continue thinking like this, I, too, am going to fade away into the night!"

It suddenly struck me how Patty would be coping with this situation if she were in my shoes. She was someone who watched the movie "Beaches" no less than 20 times and balled like a baby every time she watched it. I figured the least I could do was give myself a break for a feeling a little "off" on the first anniversary of her death. Regardless of what I expected (or hoped) would happen on this night, I realized I had to accept the way it was. If I was going to experience any peace at all, I needed to accept everything from the way I felt, including the dismal sky, and that even though a whole year had passed, it was still so hard to let Patty go.

I heard a voice within me say I was exactly where I was supposed to be. By now, the band had already started to play, and I decided to join my friends in the festivities around us. As I looked at the girls, I realized there was no better sign of Patty's presence than being in the company of each other. The five of us danced and carried on in the same way as if Patty were with us. Staring into the open sky, I felt blessed as I took it all in.

In an instant, it was clear to me that I didn't have to find Patty in a sign, but rather in a true moment of peace within myself. I finally found what I was looking for in that sunset. I realized it was peace that I had hoped to know on Patty's anniversary. And in that moment, I did.

"You are with me," I said out loud, so touched by the moment. It was 7:45 p.m.

My friends and I all hugged and raised our drinks in honor of our friend, Patty. There was a feeling of love all around us. You could see it in the way we celebrated each other. It was because of both Patty's life and death that we grew to love each other that much more. As I looked at my friends, Patty never seemed more with us. It was a feeling all of us knew.

There was something else, however, that was becoming even more apparent. The song the band was playing was "Dear Prudence" by the Beatles. The first time I heard my friend's band play the song, which was shortly after Patty died, I had felt an instant connection. Maybe it was hearing the lyrics, "You are a part of everything." More than that though, it was Patty's presence I felt when I heard those words. It was one of the special songs that I claimed I would always know as a sign of Patty. I couldn't believe that I was hearing it now.

I was overwhelmed as my friend sang the words. As the song continued to play, the music translated every emotion I felt inside. It was the communication of love, knowing, and meaning that words can never say. At that moment, I felt such peace. It was then that I turned my head to the west only to see a bright orange ball sinking into a pink and purple sky.

I was in total disbelief of what I was seeing. Amazed, I started walking towards this beautiful scene and without a doubt a sign from Patty. As I walked towards the sunset with the music of my friend's guitar solo as the symphony to my moment, I realized that I couldn't have thought of anything so beautiful in all my life. It was a moment that promised so much life, as Patty and I said our own last good-bye. I felt the most awesome and profound sense of love that could never be felt without loving someone enough to say good-bye; loving them and yourself enough to let them go. It becomes the chance you must take, so that you both can move on.

"I let you go, Patty," I said through my tears as I stared into the horizon.

"Thank you, thank you, thank you for everything you've given to me in this life. Go where you need to go, and be who you need to be. I want you to be happy and to be where you belong." I silently affirmed this to Patty, promising to let her go as I watched my pain fade into the setting sun.

*   *   *

Death is a natural part of life. Grief is just as much a part of this process. Despite all the hope and signs I am continually touched by, healing has taken time. I know a part of me will miss Patty forever. To this day, I still give myself room for feeling that loss. However, it is when I find myself suddenly smiling that I know her spirit is near. You feel the love that was known, which heals the loss. I see her in a sunset, a sunflower, a song, my own act of acceptance, and at the end I see her smiling. Every one of those times I find myself uttering the word "amazing."

"Life, living, and you, Patty. Thank you, thank you, thank you!"

Those words come so naturally, like she is standing right next to me. Once again, my friend and I have shared a moment as true as when she was alive. She is there like the rainbow after the storm, greeting the glow I now feel within myself. After the clash of darkness and light comes this beautiful rainbow. Patty always loved rainbows. She would think of her father, and she once thanked me for helping her to see them.

It would be nice if the story ended there. A story inspired by life's spiritual lessons leads to an enlightened life. However, once we have learned these lessons, life doesn't stop challenging us to grow. My picture convinced me that life is a spiritual journey. But as I found out, it inspired another purpose. Through the process of knowing days that didn't seem like there might be another, that purpose began to unravel.

As much as I was learning many spiritual lessons, I was struggling emotionally to get my life on track. What seemed like such a hard thing to go through after Patty died became even harder. Five months to the day after Patty's death, on December 3, 1995, one of my brother's best friends was killed. Ethan was tragically caught in the middle of a random act of violence and lost his life at 21 years old. Both Patty and Ethan were people who lit up the room and were loved so much. It was because of both of their deaths, that the world felt like a very dark place.

Throughout that time, I would often stare into the angel I saw in my picture, searching for insight. In terms of my personal life, I wanted to stand by the answers I thought I knew. I wanted to possess the courage Patty had challenged me to know. I wanted to be strong despite my fears and live true to myself. I had no idea how hard it would be to do this.

As I see it all now in panoramic view, a series of events makes sense. I see myself living at the mercy of my fragile emotions. I didn't realize I was in this place when I accepted my then-boyfriend's marriage proposal seven months after Patty died. This decision seemed like the perfect way to know happiness again. I was not looking towards the future and all the things I wanted in life. At the time, the security I found in my relationship was enough for me; until I realized it wasn't.

The year after I got married, my life was not the way I expected it would be. I felt like I was living on another planet—so far away from the life I wanted to be living and nowhere close to living the life I knew before Patty died. Despite this, I was determined to find my way again. However, my determination was simultaneously upstaged by a series of difficult circumstances—more than that, by a series of choices I made based on fear.

It was while I walked down that road of fear that I realized no matter how badly I wanted my life to change, or could see the life I wanted in the distance, fear was not going to get me there. Through that path, I learned a series of little lessons, which became the greatest lesson of my life: "Regard your life, and it will regard you."

If this becomes our one true intention, the rest will fall into place. It was one of the first principles I learned through my friendship with Patty. Living from a place of fear kept me from anything but regarding my own life. Through the next five years of asking myself, "Why is this happening to me?" I finally came to understand what it means to "regard your life and it will regard you."

I finally asked myself certain questions, such as why I married someone who I loved but knew in my heart would not be right for me. Why I chose to continue in a devastated marriage when I felt I was dying inside. Why I allowed myself to live at the mercy of someone else's dysfunctions until they became my own. Why I left and why I came back. Why the pregnancy of my first child was one of the most challenging experiences of my life. Why after my child was born, the roller coaster ride of someone else's addiction had reached its peak. Why I would be diagnosed with breast cancer three days before my 29th birthday. Why my marriage no longer became a choice, but a decision of practicality, why that decision threatened every practicality and stability I knew. Why every time I made the choice to end my marriage, I seconded-guessed myself into believing that my choice to move on was selfish. Why I know now that life never works, no matter what our efforts may be, without facing the truth of why it isn't.

Throughout those years, I held on to the belief that things would change if only I could uncover the rock that hid the magic answer. I prayed, read books, confided in friends, and affirmed every positive word I could fathom. I kept asking myself, "What is the lesson?" It's not something you want to ask when you're feeling desperate, even though it may be the only hope of changing that desperation.

As someone once said to me as we were discussing my past and the state my life had become, "Oh I see. You thought you would never have to feel bad again?"

Well, maybe not so much "bad." But I thought the worst was behind me. It wasn't just Patty's death I was trying to move on from. It was the first twenty years of my life that I couldn't stop seeing in the rearview mirror. I'm not suggesting that I thought we ever stop learning in life. But it seemed that so many challenging circumstances were happening at once. I guess it was true that I wanted only good things to happen, where difficult choices were no longer necessary.

As I worked to turn my life around, I thought the day would finally come when I would understand the lesson of what I should have done, or what I could have done differently. It would be the experience of knowing that one glorious moment, when everything scattered comes together. I wanted nothing more than to figure out where the hell I had gone wrong. To my surprise the realization that came to me was something else altogether. I learned that perhaps I was looking to find the wrong answer. Self-responsibility is one thing—self-punishment is another.

A lesson usually implies something we've learned from an experience or choice we've made. Yes, some choices we make are based on fear. But who says the things we've chosen to do are not meant for us? Who says there is not Divine purpose in failure or what we fail to do for ourselves? Even at times when I knew better, there was something else that called me to experience it. Without that force, I wouldn't have stayed married long enough to bring my child into this world. That Divine force became clear when my daughter's life was given to me on my 28th birthday. It was the paradox of any lesson I thought I failed to know.

Patty used to always say to me, "You are so strong." I never considered myself strong. My reply to her was, "I don't really see too much choice in the matter." I guess, though, there is always choice. We prevail over hardships realizing we are strong, not because of what faces us, but because of how we choose to face it.

Patty inspired me to see the struggles I faced in life as a journey of enlightenment. She never told me what to do or judged me for what I didn't get right. It was one of the things I missed most about her. I missed the enthusiasm, validation and positive reinforcement that Patty always shared with me. My path now was to embrace the same sense of confidence through the words I would tell myself.

The miracle was before my eyes. The beautiful, strong, and confident spirit I saw in my picture reflected every truth I learned during my friendship with Patty. "Here it is.

It's real," I told myself.

The question is, "What will you choose to do with it?" I could hear Patty asking me.

Something told me that I had to be open to the way in which God would answer my prayers. I kept hearing from one friend, "This is your life and only you have the power to make it what you want it to be." I interpreted that to mean I needed to make certain choices. The Universe would not bring the better life I desired if my choice to truly live it wasn't mine.

"Is this really the answer? Is it all about choices?" I asked myself. If that was so, the only thing left to do was to pray for the courage to make them. I realized then that it was never unclear to me what I wanted in my life. It was the courage part that at times felt so difficult.

I shared this realization with a friend of mine, and I was excited to hear that she too was in a place in her life that required the virtue of courage. It was a beautiful conversation and together, we realized we both needed courage to take the steps we wanted to take in our lives. A few days later, a cousin of mine gave me an "affirmation" or "power bead" bracelet for my birthday. This bracelet represented the power of "courage."

"Well, I guess that says it all," I said to myself. For me, it would take every bit of courage to listen to my heart. The blessing was that I had been down this road before. I knew the choices I needed to make. Despite how I afraid I was, I needed to make them. More than that, I needed to believe that whatever choices I made, spirit was on my side. As I remembered my conversation with Patty the last time she was home before she died, "Because you are committed to living the life you know you are supposed to be living is why we take that chance."

The fact of the matter was, I had tuned out my inner voice and simply hoped that everything would work out okay. However, our spirit will always be the pang in the gut saying what is or what isn't right for us. Much like unhappiness, depression, anger and anxiety, it is the battle between our psychological fears against our spirit's fearlessness. It is the clarity versus the confusion.

I know I have come a long way from the time when things felt the lowest in my life, when I allowed circumstances to consume me. There was a time when I only focused on the drama happening before my eyes. However, when my daughter was born, I decided to focus my energy only on the joy of her new life. I wasn't going to miss a minute of it. I was determined to give her the very best life I could starting from day one. I realized then that where we focus our energy is what creates our experience. For the sake of my daughter and for the sake of myself, I knew that mine could no longer be compromised.

I can only attest from my own experience that life is a spiritual journey. Everything has its purpose. We all have felt what it means to live in fear, confusion, frustration, hurt, and to long for something better. It is the flux of life. The downtimes can last for months, even a period of years. It is through our struggles, however, that we learn our greatest life lessons. For me, this truth was never more apparent than when I was in Colorado standing alongside the Arkansas River at Patty's memorial service, where I took a picture of one of the most awesome sights I have ever seen. It is the reflection of a miracle that I see in my picture that inspires me to see beyond my fears.

I believe the hardest lesson is that there are many ways in which we are challenged to learn. I know now it's my choice to determine what those lessons will be. I know that when we are ready to move on from experiencing certain struggles, we will. When we are ready to experience joy in our lives, we do, and when we are ready to make certain choices, we'll have the courage to make them.

After years of going through this journey, I realized there is no single answer that describes life or death. It is so much deeper than that. I could never define what it means, only that there is meaning. There is no easy way to escape grief—it is a process. Seeing the picture I took at Patty's memorial service is what convinced me that I would get through it. However, healing, learning and growing have taken time.

I wish everyone in the world could experience the inspiration and comfort this picture has brought to me. I want every person who sees it to be freed from their pain and heartache. I know, though, that no words or picture could ever do that. One thing I do know, for sure, is that death is not an end. We don't need a spiritual medium to tell us that we are connected to the ones we love—we need to listen to our own hearts. The lines of communication are always open in spirit. As I found, the most powerful and real connection can be found when we are present in life.

We are here to experience life on all levels, whether it is through joy, pain, loss, fulfillment, happiness, or heartache. If we experience growth, then those experiences have served their purpose. "But grow into what?" I have asked myself. Grow into our truest expression, an act of God. Writing this book has taught me this.

Life is a phenomenon. It is a thread of experiences that takes us from one state of mind to a Higher one. In an instant, we can know a sense of clarity, despite so many of our unclear destinations. The purpose of our experiences can and will shine through. There could not have been one without the other. When we reach that place of understanding, we experience a sense of reverence that only a faithful heart could know.

It was during my drive to work one ordinary spring morning, a few months after Patty died, that a new thread tied through. While still in my early morning consciousness, as I was sipping my coffee staring into the open sunlit highway, I began contemplating what I should be doing in my life. I felt I was supposed to be doing "something." I began to think about how much Patty and I loved to discuss our "spiritual breakthroughs" and our desire to write them down. I thought about my picture. I thought about the way others had responded to it. I remembered the way Patty and I put everything into themes, assigning a chapter to everything that created our story.

That morning as I continued my drive, I was overcome by waves of thought and emotion that sent my heart pounding. Suddenly, it all came together. I would write down the spiritual lessons Patty and I learned through our friendship. "I'm supposed to write the book that Patty and I planned to write together!" I gasped out loud. Suddenly I knew the reason I had my picture—which to me reflected every spiritual belief Patty and I learned through our friendship. There was no other cover that could represent this book.

I was consumed by the most excitement and energy I had felt since Patty died. From that day on I continued the journey—and it was no doubt a journey—of writing "our" book. While I drove, while I walked, while I slept, and no matter how much time had passed since the last iteration, I felt like "it" continued to speak to me. However, despite my enthusiasm, finishing this book from beginning to end became its own story.

Luckily, God knows our bad habits of self-doubt more than we do, which is why just moments after I was inspired to write my book, I asked for a sign. I was almost afraid to ask in the event I didn't see one. But if I was going to put my heart and soul into this, I had to put it out there. "God, is this really what You want me to do?" I asked out loud, knowing in my heart that it was. It was at that exact moment, as I turned my head to change lanes, that a huge semi-truck passed by me with the letters G.O.D. across it.

As that truck passed by, I wasn't aware that I was about to enter some of the most challenging years of my life. I had no idea how much energy it would take to write a book while trying to manage new and single motherhood, financial uncertainty, and a lifetime filled with baggage. At the same time, I was determined to follow through with what I knew I was supposed to do. I had reached a turning point and made a commitment to myself not only to complete this book, but to resolve the way the pages of my life were turning.

From the moment I decided to put this story into words, I wrote countless pages on everything from loose-leaf paper, napkins, notebooks, and on whatever else that I could. I was finally ready to put it all together. By now I was living in a house that I shared with my mom, my two sisters, and my two-year old daughter. An old family friend of ours had rented it to us and said it would be a wonderful house of comfort and healing for us. The house happened to be only a few blocks away from the home I grew up in during the second half of my childhood, where my family lived for 15 years. Once we moved from there, my family moved into another home. Shortly after, my parents divorced and moved into their own homes. Between those years, I separated from my husband and my daughter and I moved two times. One of those moves included living with my father for three months and then with my mother as I recovered from having a mastectomy. (I'm laughing as I write this because the whole thing was totally insane!)

Gratefully, this house was a comfortable, good place to live, and at that point we were all in need of a little healing!

There, in this house, I was bound together with family, old and new, as each of us worked to make a new life for ourselves. Living with my mom and some of my younger siblings just a few blocks away from the home I grew up in, while raising my young daughter, was not where I planned to be during this stage of my life. Somehow though, living in that house with the support of my family gave me the strength to do what I needed to do for myself. It was a new beginning for all of us.

Writing this book has taught me about patience, commitment, and the act of putting one foot in front of the other even though there are more obstacles than you count to do this. I saw my life on a parallel path. I didn't know if I had what it would take for either challenge. But as I continued to write, I was taken back to so many lessons that I was searching to know again. For that reason alone, I knew I had to keep writing.

I dreamed about Patty two nights ago. We were in the middle of some random scenario and Patty was standing up for me. I felt her presence again and how much it meant to me. I felt so relieved she was there. Then it suddenly occurred to me that Patty had died, but that she must have come back. "You're back!" I said to her. "So is this how the story is supposed to end—you come back to life?" I asked her. I was so eager to hear from Patty what it all meant.

While still in my dream, Patty looked at me with an expression on her face as if to say, "What are you talking about? I've been here all the time."

I felt like I was given the answer I was looking to find. As I realize now, life is not about discovering the answers of what we don't know so much as it is about living what we do know. I believe Patty's message to me in my dream was to tell me that everything I needed was already there.

Although I'm almost afraid to say it, the chaos in my life is no longer what it used to be. My family and I have since moved to our separate spaces. It was during the final week of living together that I began the last chapter of my book. As I was taking my daughter for a walk during one of our evening strolls around the neighborhood, I suddenly heard the answer I had been looking for the past five years since Patty died.

No matter how challenging circumstances may be in life, when I have prayed for peace and peace alone, I have experienced the most happiness. Not for the bills to be paid, the job I want, relationships to be what I want them to be, the pain to end, the plans I've made, but just peace. I have always experienced a happiness that felt more certain than anything I previously thought I needed to be happy. When I look at my picture, I am reminded of the answer that I received when I've prayed for peace.

Prayers of desperation aren't prayers, rather a frantic plea that feels more like begging. That night, I realized that I had been so gripped by fear that I wouldn't know an answered prayer if it hit me on the head. I decided to let go of everything I was obsessed with trying to figure out. I prayed for peace. Whatever happened from there, would be out of my hands. My panic has challenged my faith. However, once again it has inspired me with the mindfulness of what it means to believe.

When I look back on some of my experiences, at times I wasn't sure I was going to make it through them. Years later, I know it is because of those experiences that I feel a sense of growth that I would never trade for the world. What amazes me even more are the things I've learned through the journey of taking chances, being open, and letting go.

It is a path that has led me to a place within myself that I always dreamed to be.

I've heard it said that success in life is based on the way we feel within. For the first time in my life, I know what that means. I feel more in tune to life's ups and downs and in-betweens. I know that life is about living in the present moment no matter where that may be. It's the only place to know peace. I know now what Patty meant by words she wrote in her journal next to a photograph that was taken of her just six months before she died.

"I can't believe that I am here, I am here!" she wrote.

I remember feeling in awe myself when I saw that picture of Patty sitting on top of a mountain peak in Utah. Staring at the photograph, I tried to understand what she must have been feeling at that exact moment. I know now it was Patty's state of mind that brought her to the peak of that mountaintop. It is what inspired her to say with such enthusiasm, satisfaction and thrill in her voice, "I can't believe that I am here, I am here!"

A new chapter of life for me has begun. Somehow at the same time, I have also completed this book—our story. It is finally finished, not because I was striving for a literary masterpiece, but because it has taken that long for me to master so many of my own lessons. The events of the last five years seem to meld together, creating a spectrum of color. The color is enlightening, heartbreaking, liberating, sometimes ugly, life changing, serene, and heavenly. They are the colors of life. It's the angelic figure I see in my photo that's taught me never to forget the beauty of life.

In the end, as I sit here at my kitchen table concluding this book, the same kitchen table Patty and I once sat at together hashing out the world, I am amazed how life has somehow connected us once again. This table that has been stored away for the last five years (until I could find a better place for it) has somehow found its way to me again. It tells me how far I have grown. At the same time, I am about to embark on many new beginnings in my life – new home, new job, new experience living in the city with my daughter, and free from living like I don't have choices.

As I look back, I realize that every experience has brought me here. In spirit, I feel my friend sitting across this table from me. We were brought here together to revisit old memories and begin new ones. Five years later, after everything and every place, I find myself sitting at the same place where it all began.

"Thank you, thank you, thank you! What a story it's been."

"What a moment …"as we would say. "What a life."

I can feel her right beside me as I take it all in.

"Carpe Diem" is the phrase that appears on Patty's grave. To "seize the day" is what my friend taught me well.

Girls weekend camping along the shorelines of Northern Wisconsin, September 1993
(left to right) Allison, Cathy, Dara, Patty, Amy, Michelle

Patty and I at the Chicago Botanic Garden, October 1994

About the Author

Amy O'Keeffe has spent the past twenty-five years studying the works of spiritual masters and has successfully led seminars and workshops on the topic of spiritual growth. For the past fifteen years she has served as a director for an organization comprised of the world's top women business leaders and has worked with some of the most successful women trailblazers in business. Through this experience, coupled with her lifelong interest in personal and spiritual development, she has developed a passion for teaching others about the key principles necessary to achieve a spiritual and purposeful life. Ms. O'Keeffe is a member of the Screen Actors Guild (SAG) and has been the principle voice over talent for several national television commercial campaigns. She serves on the leadership board of WINGS, an organization dedicated to providing victims of domestic violence, safe shelter, training and resources to reach economic independence. She is also the mother of a twenty-year old daughter and proud to say that they share the same birthday.